My Year in WORDS

what I learned from choosing one word a week for one year

Charity Singleton Craig

G

Glendale Press
Frankfort, Indiana

Published by Glendale Press
Frankfort, Indiana

Want to use portions of this book in a presentation or on your website? No problem. Use up to a chapter without asking permission. Just let your readers or audience members know where you got it. Want to use more? Just ask. Visit www.charitysingletoncraig.com/contact/ for more information.

Portions of this book were originally published online at www.charitysingletoncraig.com.

Cover Design by Charity Singleton Craig

ISBN: 978-0-9979571-0-5

To the Word, who brings life

Table of Contents

Introduction

If I had to go back to the beginning, back when I first started keeping a word each week, the story of *why* would feel pretty unsatisfying. I didn't know then how helpful it would be to think carefully about my life each week. I didn't realize that it would become the "thing" I'd be known for and that people would stop me in public to tell me their word. I didn't know that choosing a word each week for a year and then another and another would form a kind of memorial to the places I've been and the things I've done and the person I'm gradually becoming.

My word of the week project didn't start as a journaling prompt or a spiritual discipline. It was never intended to become a meme or a community builder. And my word of the week certainly wasn't intended to become its own hashtag (#wordoftheweek).

Choosing one word a week and writing about it was simply my way to bring a little focus to my blogging and provide a theme to my website. I figured since I'm a word girl anyway, writing about words would be a natural fit.

Turns out it was. An even better fit than I imagined. And in the process, my word of the week has become all those things I never intended it to be and more.

To create the book you are now reading, I compiled the first year of my word of the week posts from my blog. I have edited them, not only to correct typos and fix errors, but also to fill in some details and explain things that may not be obvious outside their original context. Apart from those changes, along with this brief introduction and a users guide in the back (for how to do your own word of the week project), all of the content in this book is available online.

But the beauty of these 50 or so essays existing together as they do in this volume is what they create as a whole. It seemed like such an ordinary year at the time. We planted a garden, we celebrated holidays, we watched the seasons change, and we went on vacation. But we also moved and made career changes and experienced life in all of its everyday, miraculous glory. If I hadn't been recording it along the way, we might have missed it.

My Year in Words is significant because I paid attention, I kept track, and I wrote it down. What are you missing by *not* doing these things?

I hope you enjoy this one year in words, but I hope you also take the opportunity to record a word of your own each week. The users guide in the back provides a place for you to record your word, plus write a sentence or two about why that word was important. If you have more to say, consider keeping a journal or maybe even blogging along with me.

Most importantly, if you see me around town or catch me online, I hope you'll share your word of the week with me.

Paper
January 28

He handed me a handmade card – a card his hands had made – with another folded paper inside. "Happy Anniversary," he told me. I smiled. "For me?" I asked coyly. "What is it?"

We had already talked about a weekend away for our anniversary; Steve wanted to surprise me, but our lives are a little too complicated for such feats. As I opened the card, I realized the paper inside was the reservation confirmation from the hotel we had discussed. In two weeks, we would go to downtown Indianapolis and enjoy dinners out and movies and whatever else suited our fancy.

"Oh, thank you," I squealed, as though I had no idea. "I'm so excited."

"It's paper," he told me, making sure I knew what the real gift was. "It's our paper anniversary."

"Ah ha!" I responded. Surprised indeed. I had nearly forgotten that the first anniversary is traditionally known as the occasion to gift paper, even though Steve and I had discussed it a few weeks earlier.

I saw my husband's handwriting in color pencil on the front cover of the folded pink paper, his penned script on the inside with a message of love and gratitude. I was thankful. So much love in a piece of paper. I hadn't realized.

"I don't have your card yet," I told him, embarrassed. I had been sick for a couple of days and had fallen asleep early the night before. I knew the gift I wanted to get him, and we bought the new tennis rackets and tennis balls together later that afternoon. I thought of the time we would spend on the tennis court this spring or summer and the fun we'd have together. But I hadn't bought him a card, and I hadn't made one for him. I hadn't written words of love like he did for me. Not yet.

Later that day, with still no card to give my husband, I told him I would have it for him on our weekend away. And I intended to. But life got busy, and I didn't get to the store. "Make a card" had yet to find its way onto my to-do list. Work, parenting, bad weather, busy schedules: these are my excuses. But really, I just couldn't find the words. Not yet.

A week after our anniversary trip, we celebrated our "second" anniversary, commemorating the day we repeated our vows publicly with our family and close friends. It was another opportunity for me to finally get the words down to tell my husband how I felt. I'm a word girl, after all. Tennis rackets are nice, but I needed to use my words.

The day passed in a whirlwind, however, and when I laid my head down that night, I remembered the card I hadn't made or written.

My whole life changed just a little more than a year ago when I got married. I suspect that's what happens to most people who marry late in life – or at any time. And I've worried here and there that I changed, too, when I got married. That I'd lost my identity or my ability to be me.

On the other hand, there are parts of me that I very desperately hoped would change during this transition. With a husband and stepsons to care for, I expected to suddenly be more compassionate and humble, less self-absorbed and self-important. As a wife and mom, I thought maybe I would just naturally listen better and be wise in the face of conflict. And I really, really hoped I would be a more thoughtful person. Turns out, not as much changed in the last year as I thought.

Recently, I've spent a lot of time thinking about why I want to write, why writing is a calling for me. And there are many reasons, as you might suspect. But at the heart of why I write is my strong belief in the power of words, how we breathe them out from inside of us and give them a life of their own on paper and screen, and the way they find their ways into the dark corners of our worlds – each others' worlds – and bring life to dead places.

My husband's words did that for me when he wrote them down on paper. They breathed life into me.

So, now it's time. I owe my husband some words. On paper.

Human

February 4

'm sorry." "Please accept my apologies." "It was my fault."
"I am not sure how that happened."
It's been a week of mistakes.

Actually, it's been a week of discovering old mistakes, the ones that are just now coming to light. The error I made writing the check to our credit card company. The typo I overlooked before hitting "submit" on a print order for work. The missed reports; the wrong data. The forms stapled instead of paper-clipped.

With all of the apologies I've made this week, I feel like a politician caught with my hand in the till. Only, I really am sorry.

But maybe not for the reasons you'd think. When I make mistake after mistake, error after error, the thing I'm most sorry about is being human. Most of the time, I think I shouldn't make mistakes.

"The only thing you're mistaken about is that you made a mistake," one coworker told me today, after I warned her that the information I provided might be wrong because, well, I've been making a lot of mistakes lately. "You don't make mistakes," she told me, sarcastically. As if to say, who *doesn't* expect to make mistakes?

It's not true that I think I'm perfect. I've made plenty of blunders in my day. But so many mistakes in such a short amount of time – it's overwhelming. That's why I told a few other coworkers today to let me know if I do something right.

"When you make a mistake, it always comes back to you. But when you do things right, you usually don't hear about it," I said. Not that anyone had given me a hard time about my mistakes. Nobody needed to. I was doing a fine job of beating myself up. "I just need a little encouragement that I can do something right, today," I told them. And I was serious.

Sometimes, I wonder what the correct response is to mistakes. Are apologies reserved only for offenses that are intentional? Honestly, I didn't mean to write that check incorrectly. Is "I'm sorry" appropriate when I really was trying my hardest? Like the reports I failed to create for a client. When I set up the process to provide the information they needed, I put a lot of thought into what I was doing. I concentrated, researched, and documented. I thought I had done it right. When someone calls and says, "This isn't right," is my only response an apology?

Or, the real question: Are mistakes sin?

Over the weekend, I read a *USA Today* article about a medical breakthrough in creating stem cells without destroying embryos[1]. Admittedly, my heart soared. Though I am not a current candidate for stem-cell therapy, I am aware enough to know that the future of medicine revolves around the promise of mapping our DNA and the ability to create healthy cells to replace damaged ones through stem cell research. If the new research turns out to be true, "that means for almost any person who has a medical problem, researchers could easily make stem cells from that person's skin or blood, and those cells could be a really powerful therapy," said biologist Paul Knoepfler, of the University California-Davis, who was quoted for the article[2].

But how can stem cells be created from normal, adult cells? According to the researchers from Harvard and Japan, the mature cells just need to be damaged with acid. In other words, damaged cells can create new life.

While I am not sure that all mistakes are sin, I do know that at the very least, mistakes are the result of Sin – or the result of being human. And being human these days – that is, in the days beyond Adam and Eve in the garden – means having a corrupted spirit and being born into a polluted gene pool. Things don't always work. We hurt each other. Our bodies – all the way down to the cellular level – hurt themselves. And we need to be fixed.

Now, researchers are finally getting to the heart of the answer, the answer that has actually been built into our DNA since humans were first touched by sin and first needed to be fixed. The answer: there is no healing without brokenness.

Monday, as my mistakes were being revealed to me with alarming frequency, I found myself sympathetic in a difficult client situation that normally just grates on me. I volunteered to help with another work project, even though I'm feeling a little overwhelmed. And when I realized that someone else should have caught a mistake I had made, I didn't even blame them. Remarkably, my mistakes were softening me.

Whereas one mistake might have caused me to become defensive, the barrage of errors reminded me I was human, and so are my colleagues and clients and friends and family members. And as I accept this damaged mess that is me, I open myself up to the possibility of being fixed, to the hope of healing and restoration.

As I was leaving my friend's office earlier today, she and another coworker clapped for me. I had turned in a receipt from a business purchase, and remarkably, I had done it exactly right. "You did it," they said. "If you do nothing else right today, you'll know that you did this one thing right." I laughed. In fact, I clapped, too.

Because sometimes, one right thing reminds me that being human isn't all bad.

Simple
February 11

In one of my jobs, I am a data analyst. That means that I look at numbers – lots of numbers – and tell stories with them. But to get numbers to tell stories, I have to use a lot of spreadsheets and formulas and queries – things I would think were boring if I didn't like them so much.

Recently, I needed to combine lots of numbers in one place to tell a really big story for a client. And to do it, I decided to research some really complex formulas that would automatically – abracadabra alakazam – give them the information they needed. I spent hours reading the step-by-step instructions online and implementing them in the spreadsheet. I waited as Microsoft Excel[1] churned out the complicated calculations, thousands of them over the thousands of rows of data I had compiled.

When the calculations were complete, I was amazed. It worked just like it was supposed to.

But then, I needed to make a change. I needed to run three different scenarios. I needed the spreadsheet to quickly adapt to new percentages and new totals. And it was doing it. Just very, very slowly. So slowly, that our Vice President of Information Technology asked me what in the world I was working on because my computer was chewing up all of our system resources.

Not to mention, how much would this slow process tax the patience of my clients sitting on the other end of this spreadsheet?

That's when I decided to start over. I didn't scrap the whole project, but I went back to the moment before the problems started. I undid all the fancy formulas, and instead, imagined how I would have gotten what I needed before all the research and complexity. I decided to start from simple.

And wouldn't you know it? Simple did the trick.

I often forget the secret of simple. When I set about redesigning my website recently, I dreamed up all kinds of schemes. I had layered menu items and pages with subtle, creative titles and multiple blog themes that would rotate over a six-week cycle. You like blog buttons? I created nine of them. Yes, nine. Nine different buttons to cover every possible theme.

And then, as part of the Tweetspeak author platform workshop[2] I was taking, Jane Friedman did a critique of my website. Her planned critique was actually the impetus for the changes I was making. Just before her virtual visit, in an online Q&A session, she mentioned something about keeping things simple, about maybe having just one, possibly two, themes instead of, say, nine. I listened respectfully. I think I even nodded politely since it was a video chat. But inside, I knew nine themes would be better.

I also knew I was going to be in trouble when Jane looked at my site.

Not knowing the exact time and day she would be arriving at charitysingletoncraig.com, I worked feverishly, trying to undo some of the changes I had made, and honestly, creating more complexity in the process. By the time Jane actually visited, I thought my weeks of working on the site were over. So, it was with both horror and humor that I read her critique, which consisted of two strengths of my website (which amounted to "You remembered to put your name and photo at the top. Good job. Oh, and an email subscription box. Nice.") and seven biggish recommendations.

I laughed out loud when I read the email. Basically, all of my cleverness and all the complexity I had worked on for days had to go. I wasn't offended, really. And Jane was very nice about it all. I just realized how hard I had worked to make things complicated, when really, all I needed to do was keep it simple.

"Well, I need to work on my website a little more," I told Steve. "Really?" he asked. I had been working on my website a lot lately. Within 30 minutes, however, I had made all of Jane's recommended changes. And honestly, I liked it better. My titles and headings were straightforward. The menu was easy to use. I still write about a lot of different topics, but I narrowed down the way I do it.

Complicated is, well, complicated. Especially, when simple will do.

As I've thought about it, I've begun to realize that simple is just another type of limit. When I try to have it all and do it all and be it all, I introduce complexity and convolution to manage it all. My life requires layered menu options to navigate the complicated relationships and social situations I find myself in. It's like writing about nine different themes – each with its own blog button.

But when I limit my life – narrow, focus, restrain – things become much simpler.

Second

February 19

I watch as coconut oil melts into cocoa powder to create a drizzly chocolate I can use to coat strawberries. After adding a couple of tablespoons of pure maple syrup to sweeten the sauce, I coat the berries one at a time then lay them on a covered plate.

This is the last step in creating a perfect Valentine's dinner at home. Not that it's actually Valentine's Day. The holiday itself falls on a Friday this year when the boys will be with us. That evening we'll eat dinner out at our favorite local Mexican restaurant followed by a movie at the theater the next day.

But this night, when Steve works late and the weather is unpredictable and the movie we want to see is available on-demand, I roast vegetables and boil pasta and chop a salad for a nice dinner at home.

Just like last year.

This is our second Valentine's Day, I realize as I drizzle. Relief floods over me as the reality settles in. *The second one*, I say again to myself as I remember the pasta and the strawberries and the salad I made last year.

We haven't had many seconds in our house. Our first anniversary at the end of December ended a long line of firsts. Each birthday and holiday and vacation and school event we encountered in the last 12 months was new and exciting. But it also was stressful and confusing. When two families are joined together – even if one of those families consists of only a woman and her dog – there are traditions and expectations to be sorted through, hurt feelings and unspoken grudges to be avoided, if at all possible.

Now that we are arriving at the second round of all these events, things feel a little easier. Firsts are momentous. Seconds are . . . well, normal. Maybe even boring.

I like boring.

When Steve and I first started making our Valentine's plans for this year, we weren't necessarily expecting to celebrate at home. Steve had hoped to take me out to a new restaurant we found recently. But a realistic look at the day's schedule rendered that idea impossible. Until that very moment when I was standing in front of the stove making chocolate sauce, it hadn't dawned on me that eating at home was much better anyway.

"Maybe this could be our tradition," I propose to Steve later that evening.

A few days later, I was admiring my Valentine's roses, which had stayed beautiful for days. The rich red of the petals grew more complex as the flowers aged.

"Did you get me red last year?" I ask, trying to remember.

"I think so," Steve answers. I smile.

Because these aren't just red Valentine's roses, these are my second red Valentine's roses.

A rose by any other name wouldn't smell so sweet.

Presbyopia

February 25

On Monday, I picked up my first pair of bifocals. If you see me over the next few days and I lift my chin to you nonchalantly or lower my brow to you suspiciously, don't worry. It's not you; it's me. I'm just trying to figure out my new glasses.

My husband warned me that bifocals were in my future when I started taking off my glasses to read in bed. For the last 33 years or so, I have suffered from myopia or nearsightedness. My glasses corrected my distance vision, but as far I was concerned, they left my near vision alone. Glasses on, glasses off, I could see just fine to about the end of my arm. Beyond that, glasses – or contacts – were necessary.

I remember getting my first pair of glasses with the Snoopy monogram in the lower left corner at age 10. The lenses were as big around as a pin-on campaign button, and the frames connected low on the corners and looped up around my ears. Trust me, they were very fashionable circa 1980.

But the thing I remember most is driving away from the optometrist's office and noticing every leaf on every tree, the way they bounced in the breeze, the way they cast shadows on each other in the sun. With progressing myopia, my ten-year-old eyes had been lumping all the leaves together into a giant green cotton ball at the top of the tree trunks.

For me, though, myopia doesn't just affect the eyes. Since my cancer diagnosis a few years ago, I have had a hard time seeing into the distance in all of life. In the early days immediately after chemotherapy, I couldn't even plan into the following week. Even today, in fact, I had to keep telling myself: just get through the day.

As time went on, I could see a little further ahead, but never more than three months – the intervals of my regular blood work and doctor's visits for the past six and a half years. Once I got the all clear, I knew I had a three-month reprieve until I had to worry about cancer all over again.

After three years cancer free, my myopia improved a little. I started making plans, imagining a future. And then a recurrence happened. And then another. I feared I would never feel hopeful again, that I would be a victim of cancer even if the disease were completely gone.

But God did something unexpected in my heart, the same kind of thing that has been happening in my eyes the last few months.

The leaves have all started lumping together again, but so have the words on the page. Not only was my near vision difficult with my glasses on so was my far vision. I felt like Mr. Magoo, bumbling through the house, the office, the grocery store.

When I told the eye doctor about it, he said it was normal. Patients with myopia tend to see their distance vision worsen until they reach their early 40s, he said. Then, their near vision begins to worsen – what is called presbyopia [1] – and their distance vision sometimes improves. "So your glasses are overcorrecting for your far vision but not correcting enough for you're near vision," he told me.

According to the Casey Eye Institute at the Oregon Health and Science University[2], the same aging process that causes the presbyopia – the hardening of the eye's natural lens and the weakening of the muscles that support the lens – can actually correct the myopia. Maybe bifocals are a blessing in disguise?

I still can't see the individual leaves on the trees without my new glasses, but with the correct prescription for my distance vision now, I can read both street signs and books without taking off my glasses, even if do have to tuck my chin and look down my nose a bit. And like my eyes, my heart is seeing a little further down the road these days. Maybe it's the good news I got from the doctor yesterday that my blood counts look normal, and I'm doing better than ever. Or maybe it's the accumulating days between my diagnosis and today. The more years between us seem to give me confidence. Or maybe I've been both hardened and weakened by being knocked down a few times in life. Could it be that those experiences give me a clearer picture of the future?

Or maybe it has something to do with hope, and a growing confidence that what I can't see is clearer than ever.

For in hope we have been saved, but hope that is seen is not hope; for who hopes for what he already sees? But if we hope for what we do not see, with perseverance we wait eagerly for it. (Rom. 8:24-25, NASB)[3]

Anticipation
March 4

With only one day to spare, I finally remembered to take my palm branch to church today.

Last year on Palm Sunday, after the children walked down the aisle waving palm branches, and after we all celebrated the arrival of King Jesus, humble and riding on a donkey, the pastors distributed the palm branches to the families of the church to take home.

"Put them somewhere safe where they can dry out," Pastor had told us." And next year, for Ash Wednesday, we will burn the palm branches and use the ash to mark the cross on our foreheads."

At least that's what I thought he said.

Having worshiped for years without the rites of the church calendar, I am always attracted to these new little twists in the worship service — the ones you don't know about until you experience them blindly the first couple of times. On Sundays, I now know to respond with "Thanks be to God," when the Scripture Reader says, "The Word of God for the People of God." And I have learned to walk forward and kneel at the altar to receive communion. Last year, on Ash Wednesday, I learned about passing the peace, and on Easter, I exclaimed, "He is risen indeed!" with the congregation when the pastor announced, "He is risen."

So when Palm Sunday afforded me the opportunity to squirrel away a palm branch for next year's Ash Wednesday service, I couldn't resist. As soon as we got home, I tucked it away on the top of the refrigerator hoping upon hope that I wouldn't forget it 10 months later.

Throughout the year, I've noticed the branch up there, slowly losing what life it had left in its green fronds. Once or twice, when I was cleaning the top of the fridge, I considered just tossing it in the garbage. How much ash would this one branch produce?

But just a couple of weeks ago, I saw the branch again, this time realizing that Lent was right around the corner.

"When do I take the palm branch back?" I asked my husband. He has been part of our Methodist Church much longer than I have.

"I don't know," he responded.

"I'll have to ask Pastor Jake or Pastor Michael," I told him. "They need it to burn for Ash Wednesday."

The fact that my husband did not seem to remember this religious ritual should have been my first clue that I didn't have my facts straight. Unfortunately, I missed the signs.

That next Sunday, when Pastor Michael approached to greet us, I spurted out, "When do I bring back my palm branch? I've been saving it all year."

He smiled. "You're the second person to ask me that," he said. "You don't have to bring it back. We saved some here at the church to burn for Ash Wednesday."

I felt deflated. He could tell.

"You know, not everyone gets to take the palm branches home," he continued. "The people in the first service don't so we can use them in the second service. You guys are special."

I smiled.

"If you want to, just bring it back next Sunday," he offered. "We don't actually burn them until the night before or the day of."

It was settled.

This past Sunday, we were running late for church and had just turned off our street when I realized I had forgotten my palm branch. "It's too late to go back now," my husband said. I knew he was right.

"I'll just drop it off tomorrow or Tuesday," I conceded.

I stopped by the church today on my way home from work, the Palm branch having ridden to and from the city with me. "I'm not too late, am I?" I asked the church secretary as I handed her the dried-out branch.

"No, he won't actually burn them until tomorrow," she said. When I told her that I now realized it wasn't normal for members of the church to return their palm branches, she said I wasn't the only one to bring them in.

"And this way, we know we have enough," she offered.

We shared a few Ash Wednesday stories, and then I walked out of the office and through the side entrance and back to my car.

My palm had come full circle, or at least it would once the ashes of mourning were mixed with the oil of gladness and mixture smeared on my forehead with the thumb of the pastor.

But that's a story for tomorrow.

Connected
March 11

Saturday, I sat around the table with seven other writers participating in our writing groups' first-ever writing retreat. When I arrived a few minutes late, I chuckled to myself as I walked in to a table full of laptops, writing journals, pens, and coffee. It was like my own home office on steroids.

Throughout the day we reviewed our group's shared past, planned for our collective future, and participated in writing activities. We talked privately in twos and threes. We worked together as a whole. We sat individually tapping away at our laptop keyboards.

But my favorite part of the day – which is really my favorite part of the group as a whole – was finding the common threads that weave in and out of our lives, the ones that bind me to these women and bind them to others. Not one of us came to the group by walking in off the street and stumbling into a meeting. We didn't take out ads or make Facebook announcements. We are all part of the group because somehow or another we were already connected to each other.

I like being connected to people.

::

It's Sunday morning, and my husband and I show up at church a good hour and 15 minutes earlier than usual. This isn't a Daylight Saving Time error. We've come to a different service because we have plans with my family later.

"I'll bet all of these people think we are guests," I whisper to my husband, because I don't recognize any of them. We normally go to the 11 o'clock service, so those in the 8:45 crowd are virtually strangers.

Then, I begin to see a few people I know. Two couples from my Sunday school class and their children, a man and woman from another Sunday school class we have visited. Our son's piano teacher sitting behind the organ. The pastors that serve the church in both services.

I settle in a little more comfortably.

After the service, we go to Sunday school, a Bible study combining many different classes for the duration of Lent. We arrive early, and again, only strangers. Slowly, the members of my usual class, along with others I know, trickle in. The pastor who took part in our wedding leads; the teacher of our own class offers up an answer during the discussion time. I meet someone new next to me. I relax a little more.

As we are leaving, we stop into the sanctuary to see our boys who are with their mom this weekend and have come for the 11 o'clock service. We know they are there, sitting near the front in our family's row, because that's where we usually sit. We say our hellos and give hugs all around. As we leave, people we know tease us about skipping out early. They notice we are leaving because normally we would stay. We all laugh as we part ways.

"It feels good to be noticed," I tell my husband as we head to the car.

I like being connected to people.

::

Today, as I scarfed down carryout noodles in between jobs, I picked up my advanced copy of Michelle DeRusha's new book, *Spiritual Misfit*[1]. In this memoir of finding an unexpected faith, Michelle also finds herself connected to a new group of people, especially at a time when she is struggling to feel God's presence. At one point, Michelle and her sons are handing out food at their city's food bank distribution center, and an elderly man smiles at her son and pats him on the head. The gesture touches Michelle.

"I felt something stir in my heart when I witnessed that quiet exchange between my son and the elderly man in the food line," Michelle writes[2]. She had been concerned about the lack of emotion she felt in her new faith. Now she experiences something different.

"I saw something deeply and profoundly beautiful there, something I never expected to observe at a neighborhood food distribution center. I recognized God . . . God's presence was palpable and real.[3]"

Later in the same chapter, Michelle reflects back on the experiences with the elderly man, along with other ways she has forced herself to be with people because of her faith. And she sees that it has made a difference: "I'm grateful for the God-glimpses, the flashes of love and light I see when I connect in a real and meaningful way with my community.[4]"

My soul says, "Amen." Because that's what I've been missing lately, living in a new town away from my friends and family and the communities I've been a part of for years. I've been missing the God-glimpses that happen, not when they are orchestrated, but when they are quietly observed as people come together for the things they share in common: a meal, a cause, a hobby, a difficulty.

But I have been here a while now, and time changes things, not the least of which is me.

I like being connected to people.

Spring
March 18

Now that the snow has almost melted and the sun shines nearly every day. Now that the mercury rises high enough in the afternoons to keep the coats in the closets and the daylight lasts past suppertime, the crocuses have begun to peek out through the wet soil, and the grass is greening up under its frostbit tips. I hear the birds warble in the late morning.

Spring is coming.

Every year it happens this way. Just when I thought I couldn't take another day of winter — and this winter has been worse than usual — I find the warm air and the bright light are too much to resist. Even before it's warm enough, I stop wearing a jacket, and I slip my unstockinged feet into shoes. If even for just a few minutes, I break free from the four walls that have nearly suffocated me while the earth slept.

Spring. The very word sounds like hope to me. The whole earth prepares for a resurrection dress rehearsal with her buds and shoots and blooms and seedlings just waiting to explode out of the ground and through the ends of branches. And the whole lot of us breathes again because we made it through the darkness and bitter cold and hibernation of winter.

But we didn't make it unscathed. Branches have fallen, rocks have been pushed into the lawn by the snowplow, potholes have formed, and the ground itself has shifted and bulged through the freezing and thawing. The large metal coil on the inside of our garage door snapped when the temperatures varied by sixty degrees in the span of hours. The wind blew the siding off our house in the back. Our son's sapling we planted last spring lost all its needles and now stands bare in the side yard.

We have survived, but we have work to do.

And that news sounds a lot like hope to me, too. Resurrection life isn't earned or bought, but its hard-fought and repetitive, and it requires much more effort than I ever imagined. Winter fear and despair threaten every day to pull me under, hold me down. The vernal work of choosing hope and faith and love, though, keeps me growing, thriving, and living.

On Sunday, we began making the mental list of what we need to do to welcome spring here. Trim the bushes. Cut back the ornamental grasses. Pick up the rocks from the yard. Take a load of items to Goodwill. Paint the front door.

And while we work, we sing the songs from our hearts that say yes and "welcome" and "we're glad you're here" to the birds and the trees and all the possibilities that ride in the slipstream of the geese flying north to home.

Preapproved

March 25

Because I am a word girl, things like book releases often translate to major life events for me. I've pre-ordered my fair share of books on Amazon; I've stood in line for autographs; I've carried books around with me for years while I soaked up every last word.

But yesterday, a new book found its way into the world, and my life will never be the same.

For the past several months, my husband and I have been considering what it would mean for me to be self-employed, to spend all of my working time with words. For the first several months of our marriage, it wasn't even an option. We were paying two mortgages. End of story. But when it looked like my old house might sell, and the two-hour commute even just two days a week was more than I could bear in this winter's weather, we started thinking about it again.

The more I thought about it, though, the more anxious I became. I found myself awake most nights wondering how I could possibly replace my salary by writing blog posts and doubting whether I would ever have a book deal. But mostly, I started doubting myself and wondering what everyone would think if I had the audacity to say I was going to do it, that I was going to follow my dream . . . and take my family down with me.

So, I told my husband to forget it. I would just keep working. I changed around my schedule a bit, worked on some organizational skills to squeeze every last minute out of the day, and prayed that the snow would stop.

But pursuing a dream part-time while still working and commuting and taking care of my family felt like too much. All the driving and hurrying and cramming in the writing after dinner in the evenings and before breakfast on Saturdays and gulping down toast and coffee in the car so I could work six hours in the city, then drive home and work three or four or six hours at home has been hard.

And even though we were quietly socking away a little money and crunching numbers and thinking about maybe someday, there were still all of those insecurities to deal with.

Then, I read this from Jennifer Dukes Lee's new book, *Love Idol*[1]:

Wrapped in these pages are my heart's cry and my personal fight for freedom, offered to you. I pray that together we can give up on

- *the inner critic who bruises, the mirror that accuses, and the mental playback that oozes with bad history;*
- *our knee-jerk response to try to please people;*
- *the idea that it's somehow all up to you and me, or that our reputations hinge on our own spotless performance;*
- *our penchant for self-criticism;*
- *our fear of trying because we're afraid we'll fail when people are watching;*

- *our inability to fully experience the love of God because we're waiting for proof from a spouse or a friend that we are worthy of his or her love;*
- *our longing to feel important;*
- *our appetite for being "known";*
- *our un-gospel notions about pleasing God.*

"Are you with me?"[2]

In that moment, something shifted. I *was* with her. I had received an advanced copy of the book because I told Jennifer I wanted to help her promote it. I was reading that introduction and the subsequent chapters *for her*, I thought. But really, in God's providence, I was reading them *for me*. Because I have an inner critic who's been bullying me for too long. I have a reputation that seems fragile and dependent on perfection. I often don't try because I know others are watching, and I'm far too worried about what they think.

So, someday is now. There are a hundred reasons why I shouldn't quit my job and try to make a go as a full-time writer and editor. And even though having more time and flexibility for my family seems like a good idea, I am quite sure giving up my job and following my dreams wouldn't be the first choice others would suggest.

But if there's anything Jennifer's book has taught me, it's this: if I believe God is calling me to something, then he has preapproved me to enter into that plan, regardless of popular opinion or, more likely, my own personal opinion. It doesn't mean I will be successful, and it doesn't mean I will fail. Being preapproved simply means that God won't love me any more or any less – couldn't love me more or less, in fact – than he already does.

Mastery
April 1

I rearrange the items on my magnetic memo board to make room for three new pieces of paper, each a calendar with the next 12 months printed on it, along with some simple tasks penned in my handwritten script: cleaning, exercise, reading the Bible. My life needs more structure and discipline, especially when I start working entirely for myself at home in a few weeks. So I'm trying the Seinfeld method[1]: choose one meaningful task, do it daily, cross it off the calendar each day, forever.

I have seven tasks I want to make habits, but I'm starting with these three. Three tasks every day that will help me do better, and be better for doing them. That's my plan. My goal? Mastery. Not that I expect to master seven different things. These seven different tasks are all connected in one way or another, all habits that will help me master the writing life.

I've been thinking about becoming a master writer for a while now. All the way back in 2011, I read a blog post by Russ Ramsey called, "A World Short on Masters.[2]" His premise then, the one that continues to propel me toward mastery, is that pursuing excellence in what God has given us to do provides a level of joy that money or fame or power could never provide.

Since that time, I've been exploring what it means to focus, dig in, and get better at my craft. I've narrowed down my interests (well, that is if you don't count getting married and becoming a step-mom); I've committed an increasing amount of time to writing; and I've submitted my work to the scrutiny of editors and the whims of readers.

Do I think of myself as a master? Not yet. Am I getting better? Maybe. But am I putting in the time and effort? You bet. And from everything I've read and heard, not everyone who works hard becomes a master, but masters only emerge from hard work. Period.

This week at The High Calling, we have been talking about moving beyond mediocrity. As I contacted writers and edited their essays and wrote my editorial summary in preparation for this theme, I was amazed at all the ways we deceive ourselves about what it means to pursue excellence or become masterful. The three articles in this theme each demonstrate a way we fear, shun, or try to short circuit greatness.

In "Playing It Safe Will Never Change the World[3]," David Rupert discusses the paralysis that comes when we shoot for excellence but instead land on perfectionism. "While excellence is God-ordained, perfectionism is worldly and frustrating," he writes. "In the confusion of the two, sometimes we settle for mediocrity."

Kathy Khang confesses her struggle to believe she is even worth excellence in her post, "You Are Worth It[4]." "Somehow I had twisted pursuing excellence, even receiving excellence, into arrogance," she writes.

Finally, in "Asking Yourself the Tough Questions[5]," Ed Cyzewski writes about the short cuts or the fast track to excellence we try to ride without putting in the time or effort. The bottom line? Less is more. "I like to believe I can do anything," he writes. "But that's just a recipe for mediocrity."

That's the biggest lesson I am learning, too, about being a master "anything." I can't do it all. At least not well.

In the *Fast Company* article, "The Four Weapons of Exceptional Creative Leaders[6]," Charles Day, an advisor and coach to some of the world's most innovative and creative businesses, says context is one of the most undervalued leadership assets. Context sets boundaries, accepts limits, understands the vision.

"Context gives us the ability to say no with confidence," Day writes. "Many leaders fear saying no and see it as limiting. But more often than not, it's the right answer when you're clear about where you're headed and are in a hurry to get there.[7]"

As I transition from mostly full-time employment to a freelance life that will be made up of bits and pieces of work, it's tempting to say yes to anybody who will pay. But that's the work life I am trying to move away from. On the other hand, it's just as tempting to want to invest every waking hour into building a successful and satisfying freelance writing and editing business at the risk of being a bad wife, step-mother, daughter, or sister. I fear I may have gone a little too far down that path already.

So it's not just the writing I want to work harder at. And it's not just life that needs a little attention. It's the writing life. It's the vacuuming and the blogging and the exercising and the book contract and the being done by 5 so I can make dinner for my guys. It's my seven new habits hanging on the magnetic message board.

I've been mediocre; now I want to be masterful.

Plans
April 8

I've got plans. Big plans.

Just this weekend, my husband and I finalized our plans for a beach vacation with the boys this summer. I booked a flight to Dallas for a meeting in May; I'm making arrangements for lunch with friends while I am there. Later this week, I will attend the Festival of Faith and Writing. I've been planning that trip for months.

And then there are the writing plans after my job ends in May, plans for the summer with family visiting and arranging work schedules, even plans for a small garden and a few improvements on the house.

As part of my work transition, I gave my employer a very long notice—nine weeks—partly to help them plan for the change since I have worked there a long time and have had my hand in many different tasks. And partly to give myself time to adjust to such a big change. Just today, however, I was lamenting that decision to a friend. "I don't mind change," I told her, "But I don't like being 'in transition.'" Giving nine weeks notice at work meant I would be in transition at least nine weeks.

It's not just tempting to spend the whole nine weeks thinking about the future; it's essential. I have been organizing files and typing out instructions and making lists about everything that needs to be done when I am gone. Then, I come home and organize files and type out instructions and make lists for everything I am planning to do once I become a full-time freelancer.

Meanwhile, the actual work I should be doing today is little more than an afterthought. In fact, I don't give much thought to today at all until I finally lay my head on the pillow. Just for a moment, I might talk with my husband about the events of the day. Then, I reach over to set the alarm and immediately start thinking about tomorrow and its plans.

I've got plans, but if I'm not careful, my plans will have me. I like to look ahead, to connive and anticipate. Half the fun of a vacation is imagining what we'll do there on the beach, wondering if it will rain, researching fun activities nearby. Planning for my new work life is exhilarating and energizing. Even planning for upcoming work trips – packing clothes, making food, arranging for Tilly's care – feels productive and important. But so much of my life these days is about what is coming, what's ahead. And I'm afraid if I'm not careful, I'll miss right now. That I might forget what a gift today is.

Sometimes, planning ahead creates those "right now" moments, though. This past January, I bought my husband a tennis racket as an anniversary gift. Actually, I bought him two tennis rackets. One is pink. (I mean, the guy has to play with someone, right?)

We schlepped home the tennis rackets and a can of balls and tucked them away in the closet, planning for a day when the sun would shine and the temperature would be warm enough to play. But it kept snowing and snowing and snowing. It snowed so much, in fact, I almost forgot about the tennis rackets.

Over the past couple of weeks, though, on three different occasions, we finally pulled them out, and though we had a million other things we could be doing – it's Spring, after all, the season when everything needs to be done at once – we drove to the court and played tennis. For a few minutes, we enjoyed right now – even though I lost every game.

I've got plans, all right. But I've also got right now. And sometimes, right now wins.

Misfit

April 15

Every year during high school, I went to a spring youth conference at Taylor University, where I would later graduate with a bachelor's degree. I discovered the conference after some older friends had gone to college there and invited me to attend. It was a place to connect with other Christian teenagers, to experience college life for a weekend, and to connect with God.

Sometimes, though, connecting with God seemed a little less obvious than the motivating speakers, the small group leaders, and even the other teenagers made it seem. When I wasn't checking out the good-looking Christian guys, I did everything I could to feel that connection with God. When the speakers asked us to close our eyes, I did. When the small group leaders asked us to share our thoughts, I always went first. Every year during the last morning session, I walked down the aisle to rededicate my life. But often during the long ride home, I would struggle to know if I had encountered God at all.

Since those high school years when I was still new to faith, I often have felt a surge of emotion or tingles down my spine or a deep peace that I knew meant God was speaking to me, however fantastical that may sound. But more often than not, when others seem so certain, so convinced, so charged up because of their faith, I find that I often have to believe without the benefit of assurance.

Apparently, I am not alone. In her book, *Spiritual Misfit: A Memoir of Uneasy Faith*, Michelle DeRusha writes:

> *When I found myself disheartened by my lack of an emotionally charged faith, I figured I had two choices. I could obsess over why I didn't feel a connection to God in my heart and why I was never moved to tears by my love for Jesus, or I could simply continue to put one foot in front of the other. I could try to figure out the next step in my faith journey and move forward.*[1]

In fact, at the heart of Michelle's story is a progression from asking "why?" about faith to eventually asking, "why not?"

> *That day in the airport I began to understand that belief in God encompasses something bigger, broader, deeper, and stronger than I'd realized, something that can't be neatly packaged and reasonably rationalized. Not only did I begin to understand a belief in God as altogether something more than I could ever fully define, contain, or pin down, I began to accept and embrace this understanding, in spite of the fact that it didn't fit well with my everything-has-a-place-and-an-order-and-a-rational-explanation expectations. As a result, I began to live more fully and freely in the 'Why not?'*[2]

Michelle's new book is available beginning today. If you've ever wondered whether belief and doubt can coexist, this book is for you.

Wind
April 30

The wind has been blowing us around for four days now. On Sunday, we noticed the wind's bluster when we rode our bikes with the boys down to the Milky Way for ice cream. In the section of the road with no houses and few trees on either side, we had to pedal hard even to go slow. Once we passed the park, though, the wind was blocked and we rode more easily.

Yesterday, when I drove past the big dump on the north side of town, plastic bags, paper circular flyers, and fast food containers hung on to the fencerows just downwind. All of creation was hanging on tight, in fact, from the giant oak branches waving brand new buds to the low hanging evergreen bows sweeping the just-green grass. A slack telephone line bounced in waves, like the sounds and voices traveling through its copper wires.

Even my car jerked hard against the rising gusts as I drove 70 miles per hour heading north to visit a friend who recently moved into a nursing home. For good. She is hanging on for dear life, too, I realized, as I watched her sitting in the circle playing beanbag toss. I was nearly swept up myself, barely recognizing her from my last visit a couple of months ago. The winds of time seem to have sped up.

See, it's been windy, and we all are just hanging on. A son takes his life. A husband lies in a coma. A widow grieves. A marriage struggles. A man seeks meaning. A woman changes careers. Tornadoes strike. Words injure.

We have faith, but we fear being tossed by the winds of doubt. We believe, Jesus, help our unbelief.

I drove home from the nursing home with the winds gathering storms then dispersing them. With 18-wheelers weaving toward, then away from me. With rain drops falling, then stopping. All the time, the wind was swirling and the atmosphere seemed volatile.

Then, I saw the windmills: tall, anchored, steady. They were responding to the wind, but not overcome by it. They moved in the wind but were not moved by it. The spinning turbines reminded me that we never see the wind; we just feel its presence, harness its power. But never do we contain it.

The wind blows where it wishes and you hear the sound of it, but do not know where it comes from and where it is going; so is everyone who is born of the Spirit (John 3:8, NASB).[1]

It's fearful stepping out into the wind, not knowing what will blow our way, wondering whether it will knock us down. But only when we let our hair blow and feel our knees bend a little can we experience the invisible power, the exhilarating presence that the wind has for us.

Stretch

May 6

L ately, I've been having a lot of headaches. About once a week, sometime early in the morning, I wake up to a barking dog or with a sudden urge to go to the bathroom. I climb out of bed, stumble through the bedroom, and realize that maybe it wasn't the dog or my bladder after all. My head is throbbing.

But the pain doesn't start in my head. Usually, I can trace the pain backward, downward, through the occipital lobe, then into the cervical region of my spine, then into my upper back, between my shoulder blades. I reach back to try to massage the area myself. It's sore to the touch.

I suffer with headaches, but really it's a stress problem. Sitting tightly hunched over my laptop day after day has meant bunched up muscles and stiff, achy joints. When work is demanding, my shoulders stay drawn up toward my ears most of the time. Even in my sleep, I curl tightly on my side, willing myself to relax, to rest, but never experiencing it.

Usually, over-the-counter anti-inflammatories can ease the tension in my head, but when I recently had to miss a day of work because no amount of medicine or soaking in the tub or lying in bed provided any relief, I knew I needed another solution.

So, I tried stretching. Movements as simple as slowly looking left then right while keeping my chin level alleviate some of the stiffness, and after doing just a few stretches every day or two for the past few weeks, the headaches have improved significantly.

Those tight shoulders and aching head are not just a physical problem, though. My life has stiffened under stress the past few weeks as I have been experiencing transition at work that ultimately will change how I do things at home and will hopefully provide more flexibility in all areas of life.

But flexibility doesn't just happen. Shoulders that hunch over keyboards become used to hunching; they actually feel more comfortable hunched that way over time, even though the position causes all kinds of trouble. My poor posture actually began back in high school, or even before. As annoying as it was then, my mom was right to constantly remind me to "stand up straight" or "hold your shoulders back." It takes creating new habits to unbind and become flexible again.

Friday is my last day as an employee. When I leave the office at the end of the day, I will work for myself. I'll still report to other people, only now they will be called "clients" instead of "bosses," and the stakes feel higher. While my work habits aren't terrible and my self-discipline is probably average, I think now is as good a time as any to focus on my work posture again, to stop hunching mentally as well as physically, to hold my shoulders back as a sign of confidence, not just muscle control, and to feel what good habits can do for a workday or even a lifestyle.

Flexibility is one of the reasons I am making this change, after all: our family and my work could benefit from having a little less structure. But if I am going to be flexible *and* productive, I'm going to need to learn some new stretches. Just like small simple movements have loosened up my neck and shoulders significantly, I expect small simple actions will provide all the structure I need for my day. I started three small daily activities a month ago that have now become habits for the most part. I have four more to add during this month after I make the switch on Friday.

And in the symbiotic way that our bodies react to the circumstances around them, I'm hoping that the stretching I do in my life will help my headaches as much as the stretching I am doing in my neck and shoulders. I can't spend too many days in bed anymore. I heard my new boss is a real stickler about sick days.

Wait

May 13

S unday night, after a three-mile run with Steve, I was
standing in the kitchen making a spinach, peach, and
banana smoothie. An unexpected feeling swept over
me: I don't have to get up for work tomorrow. Or ever!

I laughed out loud. "I just had the best feeling," I told
Steve.

Not that I won't be working. Not that I won't still be
setting the alarm. Not that I won't be driving to meet with
clients occasionally. But the feeling I had been waiting for
over the past few months, the feeling of relief at quitting my
job and becoming a full-time freelancer: finally, I had that
feeling.

Then, I got up Monday morning.

It wasn't actually regret that I felt when I woke up
Monday, but as I looked ahead at my week and realized
that travel plans for my High Calling editorial duties and a
trip up north to visit a friend in the nursing home and an
extra freelance job I took on when I wasn't sure what the
rest of May would look like, plus doctors appointments and
on-site meetings and training next week with another client
mean that the casual life of being my own boss and doing
whatever I want to do is on hold for at least two more
weeks.

So I wait.

Actually, I'm not sure the life I had been waiting for recently is the life I will ever have. I said I want "flexibility," but I'm not being very flexible. I said money wasn't the issue, but I still need to earn some. I said I wanted to be my own boss, but I'm afraid of my lack of priorities or organizational skills.

But it's in the waiting that I am figuring those things out. Had I quit my job one day and started my new freelance life the next, I would have messed up a lot of things, maybe even failed. Instead, in the waiting, I had time to discover what it is I really want.

During the wait, God also prepares me for what it is I'm really going to get.

::

I'm not the only one waiting.

At a nursing home about 100 miles north of my home, a friend spends her days going to physical therapy, eating at a table with John in the downstairs dining room, and playing Bingo and other games in the recreation area.

My friend will be 92 this summer, and though it's usually not polite to tell a woman's age, I don't think she would mind. In fact, just yesterday, as I sat in her new navy blue microfiber lift chair learning about her new life in the nursing home, she told me that it was fun to have lived this long, to be able to tell people that she had made it past 90.

"But it's also good to know that Jesus is waiting for me when I die," she said. She thinks that day may come soon. She told me so yesterday just before she nodded off to sleep sitting in her wheelchair.

During lunch, her mind had been slow but clear. After the dining room staff wheeled her back to her room, her thoughts became foggy. She asked if I had trouble driving in the snow on the way up, she talked about me in the third person, like I was someone else, and just before I left, she asked where the man from church had gone who had just been standing next to me. No one had been there but me.

I wanted to tell her that she wasn't going to die soon. I wanted to tell her that she has a long life ahead of her, and that life in the nursing home could be really fun. John from the dining room had a great sense of humor, after all.

But I know my friend has been waiting a long time to see Jesus. Her husband died several years ago. Her health has declined significantly in the past few years, especially in the past few months. And now, she's tired. She's waiting to go home.

So, I told her that I would miss her, that I hoped I would see her again before she went. And when I left, I hugged her really tight, kissed her on the forehead, and told her how much I love her.

Expectation
May 20

Last week, I flew to Dallas on a direct flight, and after that experience, I've sworn off all connecting flights for the future if I can help it. Flying direct is definitely the way to go. Not only did I have a direct flight, I scheduled plenty of extra time before and after each leg of the trip; the flight could be early, late, on-time. It didn't matter. I had the time.

Giving myself a little extra time throughout the trip changed my expectations about how things would go, and I found the whole experience to be much less stressful than usual. It wasn't that nothing went wrong. In fact, adding in the extra time was based on an assumption that things would go wrong. And a few things did: when we arrived in Dallas, our plane had to wait on the tarmac for about 30 minutes while we waited for a gate to open up. Then, after having a leisurely lunch, we initially went to the wrong hotel and lost about 30 minutes getting another shuttle back to the correct one. But none of it fazed me. I expected things to go wrong. Everything was happening according to plan.

Now, go back with me a day or two before my trip to Dallas, about this time last week when I was writing here on my blog about how I expected to be moving into my new work schedule last Monday but new circumstances were making me wait a little longer. I'll admit: I was frazzled. I had expected a seamless transition into a perfect new work life, and instead, I discovered that there were still scheduling conflicts, hour-long car trips to run errands and meet with clients, soccer games in the evenings, and doctor's appointments in the mornings. Somehow, when I imagined what my life would be like as a freelancer, I forgot to factor in . . . life.

So, as I made plans for Dallas, allowing a little extra time here and there to accommodate all the things that may go wrong, I realized the need to change my expectations about the rest of my life, too.

For one, transitions take time, and if I expect to go from employee to self-employed without a few glitches along the way, I'm going to be disappointed. But also, just because I'm now my own boss doesn't mean I get to be the boss of everything and everyone. If I think I'm going to have complete control over every aspect of my life just because I work for myself, well, I don't even have a word for what those poor expectations will produce.

Mostly, I know that even my expectations about my expectations may need to shift. I can't even imagine all the ways that God may surprise me in the coming days or all the ways in which I might feel like the rug has been pulled out from under my feet. I've been there before. I can't plan for these things. I can't live with a contingency plan for every worst-case scenario.

In the end, even the most realistic expectations can't prepare me for everything. Only God can.

So, I trust Him, and expect the worst.

Just kidding. (About expecting the worst, that is.)

Long
May 27

Yesterday was my youngest stepson's birthday. He turned 11.

Of course, I wasn't there the day he was born. I didn't change a single diaper, or wave at him on the bus as he went off to kindergarten. I don't have the first tooth he lost wrapped in gauze in my jewelry box, and I haven't been around for all of the incremental changes that come with watching a child grow. I also haven't had time to get used to the increasing dare-devilishness that he and his brothers often attempt. I hold my breath a lot.

But I have known all three of the boys for about two years, and they are different today than they were when I met them. That's what I told the birthday boy yesterday morning.

When he got up, I asked him if he felt any different now that he is 11. *Not really*, he responded. I expected as much. (Is it a sign that I am getting old that I even asked that question?)

"You don't really change much from day to day," I told him. "But do you feel differently than you did last year at this time?" He nodded. I nodded, too.

Change is most obvious when we take the long view.

Today, as I was thinking about my word of the week, I glanced back over words I have chosen for the past several weeks. Each week can feel so overwhelming, so directionless, so different from the next. But taking the long view, I'm seeing themes emerging from these words that seem to choose me: anticipation, connected, preapproved, plans, earth, wind, stretching, wait.

What has seemed disruptive and tumultuous for several months has actually been the birthing of a new phase of my writing life that I could barely dream of until recently. And today was the beginning I had been waiting for. It wasn't perfect. I slept 15 minutes later than I should. Our middle son was home sick for the morning, and I had to stop to make homemade chicken noodle soup before sending him off to school at noon. I didn't get everything done on my list, but I have a list! Tomorrow, I will tackle some more of it.

And next year, I will look back at today and realize how very far I've come, even if it doesn't feel like it on each of the next 365 days.

Growth
June 3

On Saturday, Steve and I built our garden. I could have said "planted" our garden, and that would have been true, too. Eventually, we dug holes in dirt and buried tiny seeds and root balls of spindly plants.

But first, we literally built the garden.

A couple of weeks ago, we bought lumber and screws and created two 4-foot by 4-foot boxes. Then, Friday evening, after Chinese for dinner, we stopped at Lowes and bought organic compost and peat moss and vermiculite.

Saturday morning, we made an inspirational trip to the farmers market where we bought a few vegetable plants and a whole lot of actual vegetables that other people had grown. Afterwards, we stopped at Meijer's for seeds and a few other plants. Then, we came home and got to work.

Once the wood boxes were built, we stapled weed cloth to the bottom, adding the compost, peat, and vermiculite to form a rich, fertile soil. Then, we carefully constructed a 4x4 grid across the top of the garden to complete our official Square-Foot Garden[1].

I didn't do much gardening last year other than a few tomato and pepper plants in a horse trough and a few herbs in plastic pots. I was glad to have some dirt to play in, but it didn't feel like gardening. This year, we are growing eggplant, tomatoes, broccoli, cabbage, onions, spinach, carrots, peppers, green beans, zucchini, and peas. And after the first crop of broccoli and cabbage are done, I'll swap out those plants for lettuce. If it all works out, with the 32-square feet now sitting in our backyard, we hope to have several nice summer-time suppers and maybe a few veggies for the freezer, too.

That much growth is a lot to expect from something we built ourselves from scratch. I worry that we are expecting too much. I go out every day to check the moisture level, to evaluate the stem growth, and to watch for signs of pests or predators. I know it's too early for the seed germination, but I watch for that, too.

The first morning after we planted, I noticed our new blackberry bush around the corner looked a little harassed, so we added a small fence around it. Having seen a bunny in the yard over the weekend, we automatically added a two-foot tall wire fence around both of the vegetable beds.

Yesterday, during the gusty winds and rain, one of tomato plants fell over. When I went to secure it back in the soil, I realized the stem had broken. I pulled up the entire root ball and buried it deeper, hoping the weight of the soil would hold it together enough to heal. But I felt disheartened.

"Let's leave it for a couple of weeks to see it comes out of it," I told Steve. "If not, we'll have to replace it." Today, when I looked out, I thought I noticed it standing a little taller. From another angle, it appeared down again.

I should know better than to worry about growth, though, to watch so closely that progress will likely go unnoticed. I can plant and water and weed and mend; I can make the proper placement and calculate the amount of sunlight. I can protect from predators, and spray for pests, but I can never make things grow.

My garden is reminding me of that.

Rainbow
June 17

It's Monday morning, the first day after a week of vacation. I get up 45 minutes later than I planned. The first thing I grab is coffee. I don't want it to be one of those kinds of days, but I am not very hopeful.

Before I can even brew my single cup in the Keurig, Tilly, our black Labrador Retriever, needs to go outside. She's whining by the door. It's possible she's just upset that our cat, Shadow, is sitting out of reach on the other side of the sliding glass, but I decide to honor her request. I pull back the curtains.

A rainbow.

I look around a little more carefully. The sun peeks through the clouds. The patio is dry. The air is damp, but there's no sign it has rained. I scratch my head. It's the first time I've seen a rainbow without rain.

More than likely, the rainbow originated somewhere that already has precipitation. And within the hour, a light shower begins. But I saw the bright colors stretched across the sky before the clouds came. The beautiful warning came first.

I needed that.

::

Most days, I try hard to anticipate every possible disaster. Not only do I love plans, I love contingency plans. Layer upon layer of this or that or another. If plan A fails, I have a plan B. My life is like the "choose your own adventure" book my stepson picked out last night.

But sometimes – a lot of the time, actually – my plans fail. All of them. Even the back ups. And I am left reeling because suddenly I don't know what to do.

Most of the time, things eventually work out. Even though I can be an emotional mess, I can be practical, too. I can make lemonade from lemons. I can pick up and carry on. I can look for the rainbow after the storm.

But I wonder what it would be like to drop the contingency plans and instead let Jesus prepare me before the disasters happen? Rainbow before the storm. Grace before sin. Peace before chaos.

::

We need the light shower that fell yesterday. The warm humidity that followed was like a greenhouse for our garden.

And my soul? It needed the reminder of that early rainbow. It needed to remember again that God goes first – not just preparing the way but also preparing me for what is ahead.

Scarcity

June 24

This morning, while helping my mom with some errands, an employee at her local bank branch had to confirm my demographic information before I could co-sign some paperwork.

"Is your address still . . . is your phone number still . . . does your driver's license expire on . . . is your employer still . . ."

"Yes . . . yes . . . wait, how did you know that? . . . and no, actually I'm self-employed," I responded. I felt my pulse rise a little. So did my posture.

"And what is your occupation?" she asked.

"Writer," I said, without missing a beat.

It wasn't the first time that I had to tell someone that I was self-employed now, but it was the first time I felt so confident about it. I felt like a real entrepreneur, setting out with an idea for business and seeing it come to fruition.

Of course, my sole proprietorship can't stay afloat on writing alone, at least not creative writing. In fact, the editing and corporate writing I am doing actually keep me busier than I had planned. It's funny how new work keeps coming, just when I wonder whether I will be able to make enough money for our family.

But this little business venture I have undertaken – that's what the French derivative of "entrepreneur" actually means – also has landed me squarely into the economics of scarcity. There's only so much work out there; if I don't take every job offered to me, I may get left behind.

That's the *lie* of scarcity, actually. In a world providentially ordered and lovingly laid before me by my Father, I don't have to fall into the trap of clawing my way to the top. I could do that; I could elbow through the crowd and make sure I'm the one getting the job every time. But at what cost?

A couple of weeks ago, a man I know from my previous church contacted me through LinkedIn about a one-day freelance job. It was a great opportunity to get connected with a local business. The job also would have cemented a casual relationship with someone who could refer me to other organizations in the community. But it would have meant ending vacation with my family a day early, and getting up at the crack of dawn the morning after a 14-hour drive home from the beach.

I had to say no. But with the decision made, was that all I had to offer him? Just no? It would have been easy enough to leave it at that, to casually mention that I would be available for future projects. But I also have lots of friends who are freelancers, and the opportunity to get connected with this man and his organization might be good for one of them, too. As I was writing a message to several of them to see if there was any interest, the thought crossed my mind that I could be making a mistake. By sharing the lead, I could be forfeiting an opportunity for myself. I nearly changed my mind. That's what a scarcity mentality would have dictated.

Instead, confident in God's plan for my own career and bolstered by a commitment to do business with a heart, I sent the message. Within minutes, I had a name to pass along.

Ironically, a couple of weeks later, another friend offered me a similar freelance opportunity. And this time, I could meet the need. Conventional wisdom might say one good deed deserved another. But I'm not so sure. I think this is just how friends and fellow entrepreneurs conduct business together.

Learning when to say yes and when to say no to work is going to be a challenge to me for some time. Any time I have to say no, I wonder whether I have jeopardized my career, whether I have left income on the table, whether my husband or boys will blame me for not doing enough. This scarcity mentality can become a snare if I let it.

Sarah Bessey wrote about this in her High Calling post called, "Rethinking Scarcity: A Legacy of Abundance.[1]"

"The myth of scarcity tells the powerful to accumulate and take and dominate, to be driven by the fear of Not Enough and Never Enough," she writes. "We make our decisions out of fear and anxiety that there isn't enough for us. These core beliefs can lead us to the treacheries of war and hunger, injustice and inequality. We must keep others down so we can stay on top. We stockpile money and food and comforts at the expense of one another and our own souls.[2]" I've just been doing this self-employment thing for just a few weeks, and already I can see how scarcity could lead to this.

But Jesus asks us to follow him down a different path, to remember that He is the source of abundant life, that in Him, I can do all things, that I can cast my anxieties on Him, because he cares for me.

Sarah says it this way:

As the Church, we are called to exist in a prophetic community, an alternative to the narratives of the world living out the Kingdom of God in our right-now lives. There isn't scarcity, not really: there is more than enough if we live like our Jesus. For instance, scarcity tells us to work until we drop. We've got to hustle, hustle, hustle to get ours and then to keep it. But in the liturgy of abundance, we practice Sabbath. Exhaustion and burn-out are symptoms of scarcity: wholeness, joy, rest are hallmarks of a life lived within abundance.[3]

I said yes to a project today that I'm not sure about. But I also said yes to Jesus today when I offered him my work, my calendar, and my reputation and said, "In you, all of this is enough."

Wistful

July 1

I almost missed them, the two little postcards tucked in a cardboard box full of *me* from the past. For a long time I've been meaning to transfer all of the old letters and school papers and photographs and yearbooks into more durable plastic tubs. With a few spare minutes last night, I washed off the four large containers, then hauled them upstairs and set to work.

The school memorabilia I found was no surprise to me. Over the years, I've reminisced through the old undergraduate newspaper stories and masters-level research papers. I've condensed dozens of projects into just a few binders, though I kept two entire sets of 3x5 quote cards from papers I wrote. And I've refused to part with my graduation tassels, the two now twisted and tangled together like my high school and college memories.

But I had forgotten about the box full of cards and letters, years of correspondence now stuck together with age, written to addresses I barely remember. I opened a couple of the envelopes – a college graduation card from an old friend, a get-well card signed with names I don't recognize. Then, I saw the postcards penned in a familiar script.

Whose handwriting it that? I wondered, trying to remember.

When I noticed the picture on the front of one card, the memories flooded over me: The Chatham Breakthrough. Cape Cod. Of course, it's Marcia's writing. Marcia, who along with her husband Dave, ran the Hawthorne Motel, where I worked during the summer between my junior and senior years of college.

I wasn't supposed to be in Chatham that summer. Not even Massachusetts. I had left Indiana for a summer ministry in Maine, my second summer working in the small beach town of Ogunquit. But when I arrived, nothing was ready. The church hosting me had been unable to gather a team as they expected. Funding was tight. They were willing for me to stay, to do the best I could. I knew I had to go.

To where? I ended up staying in an office-turned-bedroom at the home of a college friend and his family. Going back to Indiana would have meant no hope for a summer job. Staying in the Boston area would afford more opportunities. Temporary jobs kept me busy for a couple of weeks. Then, I learned about the chambermaid job in Chatham.

After all that had happened that summer, I ended up staying in Cape Cod only three weeks, filling in through the end of the busy season for an employee who had left early.

I spent mornings cleaning motel rooms with the other college students who worked there. We all lived together in a converted room near the motel laundry. In the afternoons, we sunbathed on Marcia and Dave's upper deck, walked along the beach, drove inland for movies, or took side jobs cleaning local rental homes. I fell in love with hydrangeas that summer and wood shingles and fudgsicles and beach roses.

The postcards from Marcia weren't about that summer, though. When I left to go back to school for my final year of college, I had decided that I would move to New England when I graduated. When February came around, I sent out hundreds of resumes to every newspaper I could find from Maine to Rhode Island. I had a couple of interviews over Spring Break, but come April, when I still didn't have a job, I decided I would go anyway. I called Marcia and Dave to ask them if I could work for them again. The postcard said, "Yes!"

Only, I never went back.

Oh sure, I stopped by for a quick visit the next year when I was in Boston staying with the college friend whose parents had taken me in that one summer. But rather than follow my heart to Cape Cod, I followed my ambition to a job offer at a daily newspaper far away from the hydrangeas and wood shingles and right smack dab in the middle of my home town. For years I wondered if I had made the right choice. Last night, as I hugged the postcards close, I thought about how different my life might have been . . .

Shaking off my wistfulness, I finished packing my memories back into the plastic tubs, stacking them neatly in the corner of the closet. *That's another project I can check off the list*, I thought, lugging the old cardboard boxes down to the garage.

"What have you been up to?" my husband asked, noticing the boxes.

"Just putting all my old elementary, high school, and college stuff into plastic tubs," I told him.

But the postcards, they are still here with me. At least for now.

Friendship

July 8

I woke up yesterday morning heavy hearted, thinking of many friends who are struggling under weighty circumstances: health struggles, marriage crises, parenting difficulties, financial strain. And me, at a loss for how to help them.

From there, I began to think of friends whose life struggles I don't even know about because we don't talk much anymore. Friends I've known from my previous church, from my old job, from other cities where I have lived, earlier churches, earlier jobs, college, high school. So many people in my life have come and gone as I have matured, moved, married. Names and faces flashed through my mind in the dreamy almost-wakefulness of the early morning.

Then it struck me: "I'm a horrible friend." I thought of phone calls not made, visits never planned, birthdays not remembered, letters never written. People I'd welcomed into my life with the warm embrace of friendship now relinquished to the demands of life, the reality of distance, the daily urgency of my own needs. I panicked.

In college, as my four years were coming to an end and friends from around the world were preparing to scatter, I felt the same sense of desperation, the same sense of loss over what was about to happen.

"People replace people," one friend had told me matter-of-factly after I confessed the need to latch on and not let friends go.

"That's horrible," I told him. "No one could ever replace you or the others." I was horrified at the thought; I hated what he was saying. People might come and go, but they will never replace each other, I had assured myself earnestly.

But his words played like a soundtrack as I dreamed of the people I have loved who are no longer part of my life, some whose names I can't even remember. Emerging from the last minutes of fitful sleep, I prayed for friends whose struggles are known to me, and I prayed for friends whose struggles are not. And once again, I released them all into the hands of the one Friend who never leaves us.

::

In the book *Love and Salt: A Spiritual Friendship Shared in Letters*, Amy Andrews writes to a friend about a conversation she had with her husband on the matter of friendship.

> *Aristotle, he tells me, describes three types of friendship: friendship based on utility, on pleasure, and on virtue (or pursuit of the good). The third type is the highest and most stable form.*[1]

Reading this, I thought about all the friends who have come and gone from my life and considered whether these categories apply to those relationships. Friendship based on utility encompasses those relationships born of circumstance or convenience, shared activities, common geography. These friendships make for great workplaces, efficient committee meetings, and welcoming neighborhoods. When the job ends or the committee disbands or any of us move away, however, we may try to keep the friendship going for a while. But if its only basis was utility, then soon enough there will be new work, new homes, new meetings to attend. And friends to be made in each.

Friendships based on pleasure form around community theater productions, traveling sports teams, even local pubs where friends gather to watch a favorite band or an anticipated game. As long as the pleasure persists, so does the friendship. But as interests change, or difficulty dampens the enjoyment, the friendship suffers, too.

The highest friendships, says Aristotle, the ones based on virtue, "require time and familiarity; for, as the proverb says, it is impossible for men to know each other well until they have consumed much salt, nor can they accept each other and be friends till each has shown himself dear and trustworthy to the other.[2]"

If it's true at all that people replace people, let it be so in the first two categories of friendship. We all understand that shared circumstances and interests make for fast friends, but these relationships can't all survive the changing seasons of life.

Occasionally, though, even a friendship born of convenience, or chance, transforms into something greater through the salt of life: salt shaken to season, enhance, or preserve. But also salt used to heal and clean and protect.

"I am not sure what it means to eat much salt," Andrews writes to her friend, Jess, "but it doesn't sound pleasant. It makes me think of tears rolling down our faces into our mouths. And Lord knows that lately there have been many tears.[3]"

These friends, even though we can't always take them with us, never leave us, never get replaced. These friends are a gift, a blessing, a safety net. These friends are worth driving for and sitting with and crying over. These friends forgive and encourage and hope. If we are lucky, we get a few friends like this throughout our lives.

::

I've been known to overthink things occasionally. Just last night, as my husband and I were going for a run, some of our neighbors passed by in their car and I spent a several minutes wondering where they were going, where they had been, how they were doing, whether or not they are happy.

When it comes to friendship, yesterday was not the first time I woke up in a panic about being a bad friend. It probably won't be the last time either. Some of my earliest memories spring from my desire to have a best friend, to be part of a group of friends. Most of the difficult moments of my life have been shared with friends. Occasionally friends have pushed me down; usually, friends help me up when I fall. And it's not just a dream-like delusion that I am not always a good friend. Unfortunately, it's true.

But if there's anything I'd rather spend my time on, it's reflecting on the importance of having and being a good friend, even though the miracle of it all seems quite impossible.

"It is a good thing to be rich, and it is a good thing to be strong, but it is a better thing to be loved of many friends."
~Euripides

Revelation
July 7

Recently, I've been intrigued by birds.
It started when my dad gave me two birdhouse gourds that I drilled and painted and hung as, well, you guessed it: birdhouses. Then, when two house wrens showed up a few days later and started making themselves at home, I became a bird stalker. That might be why I haven't seen them lately.

But after the house wrens, I started noticing other birds. The red-breasted robins that fly around our backyard and often land in the grass to eat worms. The bright yellow finches that flew along with us across County Road 100 as we drove to dinner in Lafayette. And the large black crows perched on power lines as I run past the highway department.

Last week, though, I was greatly distressed to see a vivid red cardinal sitting atop the tomato cage in my garden, head down in the plant pecking away. I know there are tomatoes there. I walk around the garden several times a week, pushing back leaves and branches to see the soft green fruit. For months now, I've anticipated the juicy ripeness of an Early Girl or Big Boy. I've already enjoyed a few firm Sweet 100 Cherry tomatoes. And now, this cardinal threatens the whole thing.

I hopped up from the couch, headed to the window, and began knocking wildly. The cardinal barely noticed, head down determinedly. When I finally got his attention ("his" because the red was so bright), he pulled back his head and flew off as I had hoped. But as he went, I noticed a fat, green tomato worm hanging from his beak.

"He has a worm!" I announced to Steve. "He was helping us, and I scared him away."

And there it was, a reminder that things are rarely how they appear. Even our deepest realities are shrouded in this mystery: "sometimes God seems to be killing us when actually he's saving us.[1]"

The next day, I couldn't help but check the tomatoes. None had horrible peck marks as I originally had feared; none had fallen victim to the bright red bird, except for his kindness in snatching the worm. I wait for him to return, though my over-reaction that day will likely keep him away.

But in other ways, I try to see differently, to wait patiently for the revelation of what I cannot even imagine.

Deadline

July 22

This week and next, I am working under deadline. A big one. On August 1, just 10 days from today, the book manuscript that Ann Kroeker and I have been working on for almost eight months is due to our publisher, T.S. Poetry Press[1].

The book is about the writing life, and with the irony that often accompanies such projects, I am working harder than ever to try to manage my writing life during this process. Last night, I finally turned the laptop off at 9:30 p.m., breaking from work only three times since 8 o'clock that morning to wake up the boys, run a few errands, and throw together dinner for Steve. We ate leftovers.

Of course during these intense days of deadline pushing, I have family coming in from out of town, and I need to make a fast trip to Chicago to spend some much desired time with my nephew. A friend I haven't seen in months will visit Saturday morning. And we've invited a family from church for dinner on Sunday.

Part of me feels like curling up in a ball and going back to bed. That's what I did for an hour this morning as I hit the snooze button over and over. It's also tempting to cancel all the plans and spend every waking hour in the office until the book is done. Neither response feels reasonable, though, not for a sustainable writing life.

I did just decline an invitation from one of my best friends for coffee or lunch next week. And yesterday, I asked a new client if I could wait just a little longer to start his project because I'm working under deadline. The hours allotted to me each day number only 24, just like yours. But in the midst of the writing, I can't stop living. Not even under deadline.

Although I've been writing about one word each week since January ("deadline" is this week's word, of course), I also have one word I've been living for the year, as well. That word is limit. It's been a driving principle around many life choices I've made with my husband in recent months. "Limit" helped shape the direction of my website. It also helps me evaluate social commitments and writing assignments.

If ever there were a limit placed on my life, this deadline would be it. The constraint feels suffocating; the firm date, menacing. What if I'm not done? What if the book's not ready? But those questions would persist without the deadline, too. They would persist ad infinitum, if I let them. Then where would I be?

I've been working with a timer today, setting short, reasonable goals so that tonight I can quit by 6 p.m. and make a suitable dinner for my husband, whose work limits him to regular deadlines as well. Before dinner, maybe we'll go running. After dinner, we might watch TV. If it's not too hot, I might talk him into a friendly game of tennis.

I probably won't get as much writing done as I should by stopping so early. But a girl's gotta live, too. Even under a deadline.

Capacity
July 30

'm sure it comes as no surprise to you after last week's word—deadline—that the word for this week is capacity. For the past few days, I've been operating at my maximum potential. I made the trip to Chicago; all our guests were well fed and welcomed. I even played a few games with my mom and niece at a state park lodge while Steve, my brother, and all the boys went hiking. The work is getting done, too. The deadline is just two days away now, and we will have a completed manuscript to submit. It feels good.

But I know that I can't continue running full-steam ahead forever. In fact, the capacity I'm operating under isn't even my own. If my life were a boat, I'm normally more of a ferry, carrying significant loads, but running short, predictable trips on a set schedule. This week, I've been more of a cruise ship, filled with passengers, making long passes with multiple stops, and lots of entertainment along the way. (Not to mention the all-you-can-eat buffet.)

I love this ship analogy, first introduced to me by Ann Kroeker in her book, *Not So Fast: Slow-down Solutions for Frenzied Families*. She writes:

Every person is like a ship, with a specific and limited God-determined capacity for activities and obligations unique to that individual. Some can take on extremely heavy loads on a daily basis and only barely exhibit signs of stress—they thrive on challenges, complications, and chaos and might feel bored if their ship is riding light and high in the water for too long. . . . Trouble is, they set the standard for others who may be able to juggle only a few responsibilities before taking on water. . . . It's hard for the sailboats and fishing trawlers of the world to say no without feeling guilty, weak, or second-rate.[1]

Add to our analogy the concept of the Plimsoll mark, the line drawn on ships to indicate their load limits. When the weight of the ship submerges the hull so the line is below water, the vessel is operating above capacity with the risk of sinking under the pressure. "If we learn our limits and remain at or above our personal and family Plimsoll mark," Ann writes, "we have some wiggle room. We can be available to each other and to other people.[2]"

The truth is, for the past few days, I haven't been operating at my maximum potential. I exceeded my capacity sometime Monday morning and kept going until last night. I was a ferryboat offering a five-day excursion with shuffleboard and lounge singers. It worked for a while. I don't regret for a moment the time I spent with family and friends, even if it meant late night vacuuming and early morning baking.

But now, it's back to the predictable schedule, back to operating at or just below capacity, back to the load limits and rhythms that really allow this vessel to sail.

Improvise

August 5

Recently, when I read a blog post by Katherine Willis Pershey on improvisational comedy[1] and was struck by how much my parenting would benefit by conforming to the rules of the form.

For instance, comedienne Tina Fey wrote about four rules of improvisation in her book *BossyPants*[2]. Briefly, those rules are: 1.) Agree, 2.) Say "yes, and ...", 3.) Make statements (don't ask questions), and 4.) There are no mistakes, only opportunities. Of course, the way Tina Fey describes them, the rules themselves sound a bit like a night of improv. And little did I know when I first read Katherine's blog post, everyone thinks parenting (and business and relationships and church and families and teachers) could benefit from the rules of improv. That's how cool Tina Fey is . . . and how cool I am not, since the book came out three years ago, and I still haven't read it.

But coincidentally, just a couple of weeks after reading about improv and trying to apply the rules to parenting, I actually had a chance to attend an improv comedy night. A group of five comedians and one musician performed an hour of off-the-cuff hilariousness at the end of a three-day business conference. My brother had invited me to join him.

As I spewed out giant belly laughs in a room full of strangers, I remained composed enough to observe Tina's four rules in action. True to form, each time a new set started, one of the comedians would step out of character, describe the scene, and "action!" In that split second, all the actors had to agree with the scenario, add their own character's story, contribute rather than clarify, and just go with it when someone added an illogical line or started cracking themselves up.

Watching the actors perform, I realized that there are probably a lot of other rules to improv, which is ironic, since the actors are supposed to, well, improvise. With the majority of my day spent in highly scripted, online information sharing (I'm not sure "communication" even applies), however, it's nice to know that I can learn how to wing it a little more effectively in my in-person interactions, particularly with my family.

For instance, occasionally, the "yes, and ..." rule is suspended. In a method called, "try-again," an out-of-character performer occasionally breaks into an improv scene and says "try again." The actor speaking has to come up with another option rather than the one response they blurted out. Also, no one person says too much at once. In an improv scene, the humor emerges from the interaction, not from a lecture. Finally, emotion is good only when it is controlled. I love it when Jimmy Fallon or Jerry Seinfeld cracks a smile or even a giggle during their stand up acts. But in improv, the scene lives or dies by responding only to the emotion expressed. Unintentional emotion can crack the veneer.

I'd love to give you examples of the ways I have mastered parenting through the rules of improv. But at this point, there aren't many. What I can tell you is we're all

still laughing here. And if we get really good, we may take
this show on the road.

Moving
August 12

We are moving.

For the past several months, my husband and I have been considering whether we should sell our house and move. We've lived here together with the boys for more than a year and a half. They lived here without me for many years before that. This is their home with lots of memories and experiences. But together, we decided to find *our* home, a place with many more memories and experiences to come.

So, we made the decision, we told the boys, and we started looking at houses. Before we could even put our own house on the market, though, we sold it. The day after we received the offer for ours, we put an offer on a house we want to buy. After two days of negotiating, we came to an agreement. Both houses will be inspected; both buyers have to finalize financing. Purging, packing, and purchasing will happen before we are comfortably situated again.

But as it stands, in about four weeks from now – just six weeks after making the decision – we will be moving to our new home.

God doesn't normally move that way in my life. He doesn't always clear a path and make things easy. Not that it's all been easy with the move, either – just fast. But maybe Jesus knew I was waffling over the decision. Maybe He knew that if the process of moving was long and drawn out I might second guess and back down. Maybe He's moving in our lives in ways we don't even recognize – maybe the house is just a small part of all He is accomplishing for us, for the people selling their house, and for the people buying ours.

We are all connected now, moved by the invisible hand of God, joined by the circumstances of leaving and seeking home.

Even while God has moved in our lives in favorable ways, I am moved by the tragedy and difficulty that continues in Gaza, in northern Iraq, in West Africa, in the Williams family, in the families of dear friends. This week marks one year since my step-dad died, and in many ways, we have moved so little in our grief for him.

Life doesn't stop even for a minute as we mourn and question and ponder and suffer; it keeps moving through the bad as well as the good. When houses sell quickly, we rejoice. When life ends quickly, we despair. In either case, we stop at our own peril. Life keeps moving.

We've started collecting boxes in the garage, and our to-do list is growing. This is what we prayed for, I remind myself, as the stress of the next few weeks begins to settle in my shoulders.

We are moving. We are moved.

Dust

August 19

I look around the office, the living room, the bedrooms – there is dust everywhere. Admittedly, it's been a couple of weeks since I pulled out the microfiber cloth and took to the flat surfaces. The house could use a good dusting. But in just a few weeks, we'll be moving. And now we need to start packing and buying paint and planning a yard sale. The dusting will have to wait.

Dust has always been a bit of a mystery to me, floating through the air, riding on the sunbeams, landing on the table with little notice. Until it accumulates, that is. One dust particle? That's nothing. A layer of millions of dust particles all clumped together? That's a problem.

My first chore as a young child was dusting. That's probably why I hate it to this day. Rumor has it from my mom – and it's possible I even remember this myself – that on Saturday mornings when I was supposed to be dusting, television cartoons sang their siren song to me, and my mom would find me lying on the floor in front of the old console, dusting the television with my feet while enjoying the latest episode of *The Wonder Twins* or *The Road Runner*. Two birds with one stone?

Dust. It's practically nothing, yet it builds up and clogs up and cakes on and obscures. Dust ruins things.

I am made of dust.

During an especially difficult time in my life when my body had betrayed me and the uncertainty of my life hung over me like a canopy I couldn't escape, I found great comfort in knowing I was made from dust. That I am practically nothing. That I am capable of ruining things. Because suddenly, it took the pressure off. I didn't have to have a perfect plan for my future. I didn't have to know the cosmic reason for suffering. I didn't have to *be* the answer to anyone else's questions, either.

In the Bible, dust is a sign of repentance. It's also a sign of humility or baseness. Dust sometimes represents the land. It often is a placeholder for the human body.

I am just dust – an accumulation of minute particles.

But God is more.

Not only is God not made of dust, He is capable of making me from dust, and you. He creates something – everything – from practically nothing. He takes ruined things and makes them whole and valuable again. But he remembers, always, that I am not more. I am just dust.

Just as a father has compassion on his children,
So the Lord has compassion on those who fear Him.
For He Himself knows our frame;
He is mindful that we are but dust. (Ps. 103:13-14) [1]

Life often feels like it's getting away from me, like tiny particles riding in the light above my head, just out of reach. Or like the accumulation of a million little things growing on the flat surfaces of my life. I can't get to them all. Dust settles in and builds up and cakes on and obscures, threatening to ruin everything if I let it. I hate dust.

But again and again, Jesus reminds me that he doesn't. He doesn't despise the dust, because He is more. Out of the dust, he raises up beauty and hope. In me, in you, in us all.

Pare
August 26

The weather forecast has included a chance of thunderstorms nearly every day for the past 10 days or so, and the barometric pressure changes that come from the undulating weather have wreaked havoc on my sinuses. Daily headaches are normal lately. The wetness also has resulted in a greener than usual August. Just last week, Steve and I were remembering the past several Augusts of brown grass and multiple-week intervals between mowing. Not this year. If he had the time between rainstorms, Steve could mow twice a week and just barely keep up with the growth.

The tomatoes also suffer from a wet August. Though the temperatures are just now hot enough for the green orbs to ripen red on the vine, the dampness is causing small areas of rot just as the fruit is ready for harvest. Just last night as I was slicing tomatoes for dinner, I had to cut off sections from the ends where they were soft and dark.

Once the paring was done, the tomato that was left was delicious. We just had fewer, smaller slices than I had expected.

The tomatoes aren't the only things in need of paring about now. August has brought us not only a frenzy of rain, but also a flurry of activity. School has started, with its meet-the-teacher nights and required homework assignments, its supply lists and fundraisers. Fall soccer practice begins in a few days, and so does church youth group. Oh, and we are moving in three weeks.

Yesterday, someone asked me if I had started packing. And I really, really wanted to say yes. That's what people do when they are moving in three weeks, right? They start packing. But I haven't gotten to it yet. I know whom we will give the two chairs upstairs to, and we've nearly picked out the desks for the boys new rooms. We also have begun collecting boxes in the garage. And I have a to-do list. (Boy, do I have a to-do list.) That's a start.

But August also brought extra work assignments for me and extra appointments and paperwork that come with selling and buying a house. Just because there are boxes to fill doesn't mean we can stop working and living.

"We'll get it done," I wrote to a friend in a Facebook message last night. "Stuff like that always gets done even though it feels impossible." She just moved also. She knows.

But it will not get done unless we trim off the excess in our lives right now. We have to still live, but our lives have to become smaller for a time while we pare down to the essentials. I'll be writing on my blog a little less over the next couple of weeks. I'm trying to wrap up a few work projects, and I won't be taking on anything extra for a while. Last week, I missed a deadline and asked for a week's extension. When the editor said, "Take your time," I asked for another week.

On the home front, we've discontinued recycling until the move is over. We don't have room in our garage for more garbage bags. I stopped dusting already, and now, we may stop vacuuming – if we can stand it.

Tonight, after dinner, I will drag boxes into the living room and start packing up books. As long as nothing else comes up.

Gratitude
September 2

Choosing "gratitude" as my word of the week is a little disingenuous. If I were to choose a word that really reflected what has been happening in my heart and life over the past few days, I would have picked "grouchy" or "ungrateful" or "frazzled" or "stressed." In fact, if you asked my husband or stepsons, they definitely would have chosen one of these words instead.

Life is full right now, and though some of our circumstances have come to us quite by chance (or providence), much of the flurry of activity has arrived because I invited it. I took on too much work; I agreed to too many commitments; I have an immature inability to say no.

Late last week, one of my cousins invited me to a Facebook meme in which I was to list three positive things in my life each day. I've seen this project circulating on various friends' walls lately, almost as popular at the ALS Ice Bucket Challenge. So I agreed. But then, on Sunday – day three – I just dropped the ball. I didn't report a single positive thing.

Oh sure, I was busy. And maybe it was just that I didn't have time to sign on to Facebook. But the truth is, I think I went to bed that night more worried about what didn't get done, what I regretted, and what I hoped wouldn't happen than thinking about all the positives in my life.

Last night, the same almost happened. But just before dropping off to sleep, I remembered the challenge, and quickly came up with three things. It was actually easy once I thought about it.

This is not the first stressful, busy season in my life. In fact, I've had months, even years, that were far more difficult. And here's what's really crazy – most of the current stress in my life revolves around things other people would love to have in their lives, things I myself wanted, too, even prayed for: a new house, an abundance of paying work that I enjoy, lots of activities with friends and family, and opportunities to serve others.

So, back to my word of the week. Rather than being disingenuous, I'm actually trying to be a little proactive in choosing "gratitude" as my word. My grumpiness, my stress, the little catches in my chest when things aren't going well – they all hinge on my ability to see all that I have in a new way. To swing things in a new direction, I need to start with a little gratitude.

While I've kept lists of things I'm thankful for in the past, I haven't been nearly as consistent as another friend who has filled up nine notebooks over the past seven years by jotting down five things every day. She's started a new online project in which she models this idea of daily gratefulness – of seeing all she's got and saying, "thank you," to the One who made it possible. And if I'm going to make it through the next few weeks of packing and painting and pulling weeds and preparing a new home, then I need an anchor of gratitude to keep me from floating away.

I probably won't make all my lists public; that's just setting myself up for more stress and more unmet expectations. But I owe it to my cousin to try to finish out the meme on Facebook, and then I'll just find a little journal, put it on the nightstand next to my bed, and ask the Lord to help me see my life a little better at the end of each day.

Today's list of five things I'm thankful for:

- Leftover pancakes for breakfast.
- A slow entry into a new day after staying up late last night to finish yesterday's work.
- Rain outside; dry inside.
- Truth from Proverbs that brings real change to my heart.
- Health for me, my husband, and my stepsons.

Adventure

September 9

Sometimes when Steve and I are out running errands or making our way home from dinner out or an event at church, he will make an unexpected turn, announcing, "We're going on an adventure."

Such was the case on Saturday after we had driven down to Indianapolis to buy moving boxes. We had already followed our noses through several antique shops, looking for a couple pieces of furniture for our new house. Since we were in the city anyway, we decided to stop and have lunch at one of my favorite restaurants. When it was time to head toward home, we found ourselves on the north side of Zionsville in an unfamiliar area.

We could have turned around, found a familiar landmark, and started again. Instead, we headed off on an adventure. We knew if we traveled far enough north or west we would eventually intersect with one of the major roads we know, plus we would be making our way toward home.

As we headed off on a hilly country road, though, suddenly things were looking a little too familiar, even though we didn't know where we were. At the next intersection, I said, "Go straight," but Steve saw an interesting sign and decided to turn left.

"This all looks really familiar," I said. "I think we drove through here on our last adventure."

"I think you're right," Steve said.

"Look, another wedding in the same place as last time," I called out as we passed a big sign announcing another barn wedding.

"Look, there's the castle-looking house again," I said.

"Yep, we've been this way before," Steve agreed.

"It's still an adventure," I said, hoping he wasn't disappointed. "Sometimes, you have to travel new roads a few times to really see everything."

We both agreed that before long we would be entering Whitestown, and sure enough, within a few minutes we were driving down the main drag. Just like before, we turned right at the stop sign in the center of town and headed north.

"Eventually we'll be in Lebanon, right?" I asked, because suddenly nothing seemed familiar anymore.

"Yeah, this road runs right into 32," Steve said.

"Huh, that's funny. I don't remember this part at all," I told him.

"That's because you were asleep last time," he reminded me. "When we hit 32, we'll turn left and it will take us right into Lebanon."

And then, I remembered. The last time an adventure took us through those parts of Indiana was on the Fourth of July. After a hot afternoon at CarmelFest, I had konked out on the way home. This familiar path was suddenly new again.

But not for long. We made the rest of the trip rather uneventfully, our adventure coming to an abrupt end as once again I began to recognize the roads, the towns, the familiar landmarks, the way home. Admittedly, our adventure was rather safe and our risk rather small in the scope of things. We have a compass on our van, we know the general lay of the land, and we had a full tank of gas.

But we needed to remember that "new" can be good, and so can "familiar," and while there's nothing wrong with taking the path less traveled, we can always find something new on the old road home, too.

Juggle
September 16

B y now, we all know that multitasking is a myth, right? Science has proven that our brains really aren't capable of focusing on multiple things at once and instead are constantly moving among the activities we are doing, what researchers have called "task switching.[1]" And not only is task switching bad for productivity, it's bad for accuracy and creativity and even for relationships.

Why do we keep doing it, then?

Not only do I try to multitask to the same inefficient end that science has proven, I also have another organizational flaw, which Steve has lovingly dubbed "schedule crowding." If I have a free hour, I think of everything I need to do that would take, oh, say an hour, and then, I decide to do them all. In just the one hour! I'm constantly setting myself up for failure.

Now, fast forward to this week. We are finally moving and doing all the things that go along with that: painting, packing, mowing, weeding, cleaning, unpacking, shopping, fixing. And I'm working, trying to keep up with client needs and book details and diminishing deadlines. Then, the activities of our normal lives just keep happening: youth group and soccer practice and homework and dinner. (*Oh, dinner*, she remembers, adding it to the to-do list.)

For chronic multitaskers who also happen to be schedule crowders, weeks like this don't go well. It's amazing that I'm still upright and typing.

But even with all the juggling going on, God is good and we are thankful. The end is near, amazingly. There is a light at the end of the tunnel – and other clichés of hope that keep me going.

Plus, my mom has come to help, which always makes everything better. She also brought some delicious homemade rolls for breakfast. After our two-week grocery-buying moratorium leading up to the move, I'm just happy to have some normal food.

Settled
September 23

The David Nevue station streams quietly on my laptop as I sit in my new office and write this morning. This new workspace is about twice as large as my old office. A bank of windows faces the south into our fenced-in backyard. I watch as the squirrels shimmy up the trees and across the fence tops. To my left, the large built-in bookcase holds nearly all of our family's books. A fireplace fills the wall to my right, with my silly dog sleeping on her bed in front of it.

The fire hasn't yet been lit, but this winter when it is, Tilly will come gladly to lie here. For now, I had to force her to come in with me after shooing her off the living room couch. We've given away all of "her" furniture when we downsized to our new home. Now, any time I can't find her, I know to check the living room where she has undoubtedly snuck up on the sofa again. Tilly sleeps there in the night, too. I found her there at 2 a.m. Monday.

We've owned the house just shy of two weeks, and we've lived here just five days, but mostly we are settled. When I tell people, they look at me like I'm crazy. So fast? My achy hips and ankles and my husband's sore back give testimony to the way I pushed us all weekend to unpack and assemble and organize. We worked hard to get to this place, and though it nearly wore us into the ground, today sitting in my office working, it feels worth it.

Last night, when the boys came for their first night in the house, it started to feel like home. Of course we had a soccer game and homework and chores – the normal busyness of life – but we also ate our first dinner here, figured out the routine for showers and the location of the towels, and slept well in new rooms, even with the creaks of a new house and the barks and roars and groans of a new neighborhood.

Since late July when we first decided to take the plunge and move to a new house, we've been a little unsettled. How could we not with a growing pile of boxes in the garage and living room, the regular disappearance of wall hangings and pillows and games from their normal locations, and the abrupt rearrangement of furniture as one piece after the other was loaded into someone else's car or van and hauled away? Things have felt a little chaotic the past few weeks. In some ways, that restless feeling preceded our decision by many more months for me.

We aren't completely settled yet, either. We have to assemble the boys' new desks and chairs; the garage is still a mess; and the weeds growing in the back yard mock me as I work. I can't wait to get my hands on them.

We also are bumping into each other a bit as we remember – or discover, in some cases – where we put things, finding our way into new rhythms of life here.

"Everything is new," the boys said last night at dinner, even though most things aren't. It just feels that way. And when our youngest went to change his clothes before the soccer game yesterday evening, he asked, "Where's the bathroom in this place?"

"In the back, just past the kitchen," we reminded him, laughing. Ahhh, the joys of moving.

But this is our place for now, this little bungalow on a quiet street in Frankfort. This morning, as I read from Leviticus 26, I took those words to the Israelites about the Promised Land and prayed them back to God about this little piece of land we live on now:

> *Lord, in our home, be present. Walk among us. Be our God; help us be your people. Place your dwelling among us. Don't despise us. Help us to stand up straight.*[1]

And I add, now, "Help us to be settled in You."

Play
September 30

Last night, Steve and I finally sat down on the couch about 8:30 after a busy day of work – the kind we get paid for and the kind we don't. For a few minutes, we planned to veg out in front of the television watching *The Voice*[1], one the few shows we like from our now-limited cable selection.

By the time we tuned in, the judges already had selected a couple of performers for their teams. The first act we caught was an earnest young man from New Jersey whose performance got two judges to turn their chairs. As we continued watching, we commented on the range of talent, occasionally discussing other things we remembered from our day, when we noticed Tilly sitting upright and staring directly at Steve.

"What do you want, girl?" I asked. She didn't move a muscle.

"Come 'ere," I said and petted her behind the ears. But she had her eyes on Steve.

"I think she wants you," I said.

"What's a matter, girl?" Steve asked her, giving her back and neck and head and good rubbing. She leaned in. Then, she ran to the other side of the room and grabbed her toy beaver tail. It used to be a whole beaver before Tilly got a hold of it.

Steve grabbed the toy and threw it; Tilly ran and retrieved it, vying for a game of tug-o-war when she returned it to Steve.

"I think she just wants to play," I said.

So Steve got down on the floor with her, and for several minutes, they played. This wasn't the first time they've wrestled and wrangled like this. That's why Tilly went to Steve, not me. But it was the first time in a while. I think Tilly and Steve both needed some time to play.

I think I do, too.

Earlier this summer, Steve and I often went to the farmers market on Saturdays. Over the Labor Day weekend, we took the boys to see three movies at the theater. In one weekend! In the evenings, I would ride my bicycle, and one or two of the boys would come along. Then, my work got crazy, school started again, we moved, and . . . well, let's just say that we haven't done a lot of playing for the past few weeks.

What does that do to a person, not playing? I don't know what it does to you or to most people, but for me, it means the muscles between my shoulders keep growing tighter. It means I check my phone more and more and more, trying to stay on top of the work. It means weekends are filled with chores and to-do lists. It means feeling guilty for lying on the couch and watching a movie on a Sunday afternoon.

Oh, and the work never gets done. Never. The to-do list still grows and the emails just keep coming, no matter what else I put off or set aside.

I need to play more.

I'm just not sure when or how, yet.

Go

October 8

I had plans yesterday, important plans for how I would spend my day working. I had a list and an agenda and a timeline. But then, I realized I was needed somewhere else, that my presence mattered, even if someone else could have gone instead. My mom needed *me*.

So I went.

Living a life of words is important to me. I don't believe that only sticks and stones hurt people. Words do, too. So I try to speak and write words that heal and offer hope rather than tear down and destroy. I think writing letters to people and leaving encouraging notes and expressing love in words is real work. Words bring life. I've built my own life around that truth.

But sometimes, the words aren't enough. Sometimes, instead of words, I need to send money or take a meal or offer a ride. Sometimes, instead of saying or writing words, I need to go and be there. Yesterday was one of those times.

Boom

October 14

Just a few minutes ago, I heard and saw a small explosion outside my office window. I was a witness, I guess you could say, but I couldn't be sure of the details. The boom, the flash. They were real. But then, silence. Had it really happened?

I considered calling 911, but I wasn't sure what I would say. "I think something might have exploded?" Instead, I decided to investigate, to look for smoke or victims or just evidence. Grabbing my cellphone and stepping into my shoes, I headed out for a quick walk toward where I thought I saw the light.

I peered around the neighbors' houses. I peeked in their windows from my place on the sidewalk. I looked up in the trees to see if any smoke or flame was lingering. Despite what I thought I saw, I could find no evidence. While I certainly don't want there to have been an explosion, the alternative seems uncomfortable. Did I really just imagine it? Later I may hear the neighborhood scuttlebutt that a breaker blew or a car backfired. Or I may not. Either way, for now, I have to be content with not knowing, with truth that is just outside my reach.

It's raining today, like it has for several of the past few days. The water pools on the patio, and when it pours down hard, a rivulet ambles through the basement toward the drain near the dog bowls. We knew that could be a problem when we bought the house.

When I first heard the explosion, I assumed that lightning had struck, but the only flash came from just over the neighbors' roof. Nothing from the sky. Nothing reaching down to wreak havoc and create the boom.

The rain blew in on a damaging wind, though, and the sticks covering the front and back yard remind me of the more common problems of storms. I was going to start adding the newly fallen sticks to our brush pile last night, but Steve said there was no need. More would fall overnight when the storms blew through. He was right.

I'll admit it: when I heard the explosion, part of me wanted a little drama this morning, the chance to be the hero and call 911. I wanted to run out of the house and find other curious neighbors, to stand around and talk about the boom and the light. To talk about how rainy it's been, and how the leaves down on Harvard Terrace and around the corner on East Street and just over on Oneil, how they all look like they are glowing.

Instead, nearly an hour after the explosion, I saw only the garage door open next door, and as she always does about this time in the morning, the woman who lives there scurried to her car and left. The garage door rolled closed on its tracks as she backed down the driveway.

The forecast says rain until Thursday. I guess I'll pick up the sticks when the sky clears.

Happy
October 22

Last night before heading to bed, I noticed popcorn bowls and juice box wrappers laying on the end table in the living room. I already had spent a good part of the evening straightening up the house, making sure mail and homework were accessibly stashed, and negotiating with our oldest son to put away the chips and salsa if he would throw away his beverage container. (To be fair, he also put the popcorn container away for me when I couldn't reach.)

"You guys need to bring your popcorn bowls to the kitchen and throw away the Capri wrappers," I announced to the other two boys, no longer willing to negotiate. They hesitated, they groaned, but eventually they shuffled into the kitchen and put their things away.

We need a better system for the clutter that accumulates around us. Otherwise, I spend a large part of every evening cleaning up after the high tides of pre-teen and teenage boys that leave trash and laundry and toys and ear buds scattered in their wake.

We'll figure it out, eventually. We did, after all, solve the towel-on-the-floor problem.

At our old house, I would often go upstairs after morning or evening showers and find wet towels mingled with smelly clothes strewn across the boys' bathroom floor.

The only time we didn't find such a mess was when we remembered to say, "Don't forget to bring down your towel and clothes when you're done."

At our new house, we solved the problem. We put a laundry basket in the bathroom! Now, the wet towels and dirty clothes end up in the basket, and I haven't once had to ask that they be picked up off the floor. Why did it take a new house to arrive at such a simple solution?

It's like the sidewalks from my college days. When I was a student at Taylor University, students often took shortcuts through the grass. But so many students eventually started bypassing the walkways that soon the grass was worn away and replaced with a dirt path, muddy when it rained. University officials were unhappy. Announcements were made about walking in the grass. Ambling was allowed, tramping was discouraged. Rumor had it that one grass-loving accounting professor threatened to lower the grades of anyone caught walking deliberately through the lawn.

What could be done to solve the problem?

The next year, we returned to campus to find a new sidewalk where the muddy path had been worn. A simple solution. Why didn't we think of it sooner?

In my life, many things are going well. In my spiritual life, family, church, neighborhood, friendships, and work, I am experiencing growth, finding fellowship, enjoying success, and solving problems. I spend big parts of every day happy and satisfied.

But at the same time, some things just aren't working. I am not as patient as I'd like; I don't communicate well sometimes; I don't see my friends very often; I don't know most of my new neighbors; I don't get as much done as I want during the day; I have to turn off the light in one sons bedroom every day. And this is just the list I'm willing to share. There are others.

Some things I can change. And I do. Some things I can change, and I don't realize it yet. Some things just can't be changed. And no matter how many solutions I come up with, no matter how many things I tweak and adjust, I'm stuck.

Or maybe I'm not.

Not too long after the university added a sidewalk to replace the grass path, students began bypassing that sidewalk, too, wearing another path in the grass to create yet a shorter cut to class. Was another sidewalk the answer?

If I remember correctly, the facilities crew did add another sidewalk or two, just enough to keep most of the students from tramping on the grass. Those who continued weren't enough to wear new paths.

And in the end, there was enough grass for ambling for everyone.

I couldn't help but think of the Serenity Prayer that has become a staple of 12-step programs and inspirational posters, the prayer first penned by Reinhold Niebuhr in a 1951 magazine article[1], that actually goes beyond the stripped-down popular version.

God, give me grace to accept with serenity
the things that cannot be changed,
Courage to change the things
which should be changed,
and the Wisdom to distinguish
the one from the other.
Living one day at a time,
Enjoying one moment at a time,
Accepting hardship as a pathway to peace,

Taking, as Jesus did,
This sinful world as it is,
Not as I would have it,
Trusting that You will make all things right,
If I surrender to Your will,
So that I may be reasonably happy in this life,
And supremely happy with You forever in the next.

It's not just the serenity and the wisdom that are important here. It's also the grace. And it's not just accepting that's important, but the trusting and the surrender.

And truly, it's not just about being reasonably happy. It's about one day being supremely happy with Him forever.

But we have this treasure in jars of clay to show that this all-surpassing power is from God and not from us. We are hard pressed on every side, but not crushed; perplexed, but not in despair; persecuted, but not abandoned; struck down, but not destroyed. We always carry around in our body the death of Jesus, so that the life of Jesus may also be revealed in our body. For we who are alive are always being given over to death for Jesus' sake, so that his life may also be revealed in our mortal body. So then, death is at work in us, but life is at work in you. (2 Cor. 4:7-12)[2]

Surprise
October 28

Just last week as Ann Kroeker and I were talking with our publisher, L.L. Barkat, about how to get the word out about our upcoming book, the words "secret" and "surprise" and "idea" and "early" kept coming up. What if we just published the book early and didn't tell anyone?

We all liked the idea, actually. It would be like letting the little book find its way in the world naturally as people discover and hear and share.

But what we didn't realize is that the surprise was really for us! Without saying a word, our publisher flipped the switch to publish our book and make it available to the world sometime over the past few days. Then, she told lots of our friends about the news, still without letting us in on our own secret. Her plan: as soon as Ann or I discovered that the book was available, she would have everyone who knew about it start sharing the news on social media, congratulating Ann and I, and surprising us like crazy!

Just as predicted, yesterday I stumbled onto the live Amazon page after following a link at the bottom of an article. I blinked, did some clicking around, and realized the book was available. I texted Ann. I emailed L.L. And within an hour or so, the notifications from Facebook started pouring in. I had "secretly" started slipping the Amazon

URL onto our various online places and updating the official publish date to October 24, 2014 – which happened to be my birthday. When I saw the first notification on social media, I thought I had accidentally broadcast the news, when in fact, a friend was the one broadcasting the news to Ann and me. The book is here!

My laptop went wild with dings and pops, the little Facebook notification number reaching up into the 90s at some points. Throughout the evening, friends and family chimed in congratulating us on the book's launch, the launch that was supposed to be secret.

Turns out it actually was.

Ann and I have a few surprises of our own to share over the next few months as we watch this little book find its way into the lives of many writers. We wrote it because we want to see writers at all levels find their way to what's next, because we really believe there is a "what's next" for all writers at all stages. This book started out as a workshop a year ago, when twelve women joined us for twelve weeks to see where their writing lives would go. The biggest surprise of all was how much Ann and I were encouraged to take our own next steps.

Many of you reading this are not writers. Some of you may secretly want to be, and if so, then our book has something for you. But even if not, the book may have something for you as you discover more about the writing lives of its authors. Or the book may have something to offer you as you explore how to take the next step into your own passions and interests. At the very least, the book offers a way for you to encourage the writers you know to walk bravely into the surprises awaiting them in their own writing lives.

I'm not usually one for surprises. I like to have a plan and a map and a to-do list. I like to know where I'm going and what I'll be doing when I get there. But yesterday made me laugh and marvel and appreciate all the ways the best surprises are the ones that remind me of the people who make the writing life worth it.

Including you.

Stumble

November 4

On Halloween night, the first trick-or-treaters arrived at the same time as the pizza man, and while I was running this way to hand out the M&Ms and Skittles and that way to get the cash for a tip, my festive Halloween socks, pulled out once a year for such occasions, betrayed me. My feet slid out from under me, and I landed with a thud on my knees.

I moaned. Steve expressed appropriate concern, though I'm sure he would rather have laughed.

"I need to slow down," I said, to no one in particular.

On the way back to the door to retrieve the pizza, I grabbed a back of peanut butter M&Ms, and handed it to the delivery driver, along with the last $4 in my wallet. Thankfully, the pizza was paid for with plastic.

The tumble through the living room was just about the last straw after a frustrating day of work and a to-do list that had mushroomed out of control. Though I recognize my work and home office and writing opportunities as real gifts most of the time, I would have given it all up, I fear, if someone would have offered me a stress-free weekend with a massage and a nap. It would have been a fool's trade, but that's where I had stumbled.

With this new week going about the same, I keep thinking there has to be a place for common sense when the pressures of life – even a good life – come pressing in hard. No one can work 12 hours a day or seven days a week for long without getting tripped up. And I definitely can't work all the time and expect that I won't get behind on housework, out of touch with the boys, or unreasonable with my husband. They love me anyway, but they didn't sign on for this craziness.

Yesterday in an email to Ann, I confessed that I was about to self-destruct. She kindly told me to take a deep breath. It's what I tell the boys when they aren't being rational. I needed to hear those words back. And last night, just before slipping into bed, I was reading Proverbs 3. Solomon says something similar: "Keep sound wisdom and discretion." Or, in other words, be reasonable, woman! Doing so keeps us from being afraid, it helps us sleep, it makes us confident in the Lord, he says.

And interestingly enough, it will help us not to stumble.

I was tempted to ask, *Where was Solomon when I needed him?* thinking of the literal fall that left me with stiff knees five days later. But the truth is, He got to me just in time. I haven't self-destructed yet. I haven't completely blown it with my family or friends. I haven't stumbled too far off the path.

And today, things are looking up.

Sky
November 11

Heading out in the car last evening, Steve and I discussed the errands we were running and the restaurant where we would have dinner and the difficulties of adjusting to Daylight Saving Time. But when we turned onto State Road 28, heading west toward the interstate, all I could think about was the sky.

The sun was setting, and the clouds hung low and light, stretching this way and that across the expanse of indigo and magenta and azure. As we traveled at 55 miles per hour, the pinks intensified over the other hues, and the sky transformed into a marquise tourmaline I wanted to mount on a ring and keep forever.

We kept talking at we drove, though I interrupted again and again. "Look at the sky," I entreated my husband. "It's just so beautiful."

This morning, working at my desk in front of the south facing window, I couldn't help but see the sky again, casting a blue and gray marbled background for the silhouette of the empty trees as the sun made its daily rounds. The wind blustered around our fenced-in yard, leaves swirling and branches swaying. And high up in the sky, the scene shifted minute by minute.

Skies like these mean change is coming. Cool dry air riding down from Canada makes it easier for our eyes to collect more colors of the spectrum during the morning and evening hours when the atmosphere is so dense. Those cold winds also usher in winter, and soon, we'll hunker down to stay warm and ride out the months of darkness.

"I'm not ready for winter," my husband said as we saw snow in the forecast for Sunday.

"Me neither," I said, though secretly I need a bit of what winter has to offer.

Change is coming, the skies announce. And outside we feel it. But change is coming for us inside, too. Cold, damp, and dark does something to a person, and we needs skies like these to shine ever brightly in those seasons.

You see, it's not just autumn when the skies shine so brilliantly. We can look up all winter long, when the bright light of hope shines brightest against the darkness.

Voice
December 2

I lost my voice," I croaked to a small gathering of writers who had come to a workshop Ann Kroeker and I were leading in Round Rock, Texas. We all chuckled at the irony, because though I was referring to my years as a newspaper reporter when I felt my unique perspective was lost in the news cycle, I literally had lost my voice that morning to laryngitis. I spent the day straining into a microphone to communicate anything at all.

We had organized the workshop to coincide with the release of our new book, *On Being a Writer.* Though we weren't sure the book would be available at the time, Ann and I were both going to be in Texas, and we didn't want to miss the opportunity to encourage writers we might not otherwise meet. As I gulped down cupfuls of tea with lemon throughout the morning just to be able to speak in a loud whisper, Ann also struggled with a food allergy reaction and fatigue from weeks of stress. We had a rough go of it.

But for that workshop, it didn't matter too much because the real work of the day was inviting the participants to interact with each other, to share their own successes and failures, to inspire each other with their own unique perspectives. Our voices, Ann's and mine, were just two among many.

I may have missed this important element of the day had I arrived with full-timbred tonsils and the strong sense of self-importance that healthfulness might otherwise have lent.

Truth is, I lost my voice for most of the whole week I was traveling around Texas. I squeaked my way through, but in one setting after another – sightseeing in Austin, a basketball game at Texas School for the Deaf, The High Calling Retreat at Laity Lodge – the stuffy feeling between my throat and ears and the threat of a coughing fit that would require leaving the room kept me quieter than usual. I listened more. I asked raspy questions and then waited for answers.

Not being able to speak helped me hear better.

Sunday morning after the workshop, I temporarily had no voice at all. None. I mouthed necessities to my hosts, Jon and Shelly Bergeron, and I nearly stayed home from church out of embarrassment. Wouldn't it be awkward for other people to ask me questions when I couldn't answer them? But staying home would mean I would miss Food Truck Sunday, and where but Austin, Texas, do churches invite box trucks serving Asian noodles and Southern barbecue to set up in the parking lot after the services? I had to go.

As I walked into the high-school-gymnasium-turned-sanctuary for the morning service, suddenly I could speak just a little. It wasn't much more than a whisper, but I could respond if needed. I found a seat as Shelly caught up with friends, and as a woman approached me, I mustered strength in my sore vocal chords. When she spoke though, I still couldn't respond, because her words were formed with hands, not throat, and she listened with her eyes, not ears. I shouldn't have been surprised. We were sitting in the sign language section, after all, where the music, announcements, and sermon would all be interpreted into

American Sign Language (ASL). Jon and Shelly have two sons who are deaf; ASL is their primary language at home.

I smiled and shrugged to the woman, trying to communicate with gestures and signals. Unfortunately, I don't speak ASL. After all my concern that morning that I wouldn't be able to communicate, I understood in that moment that this woman faces the loneliness of having no voice most days. At least in the sign language section at church, she thought she would finally be heard. When she encountered me, she was wrong.

When Shelly rejoined me, I told her about the encounter, how horrible I felt that I couldn't communicate.

"Will you tell her I'm sorry?" I asked, hoping Shelly's hands could be my voice. "Tell her that I don't speak ASL, that I'm sorry I didn't understand her."

Later that night, I joined a group of women for a "Friendsgiving" dinner. As the night went on, my voice got weaker and weaker. Ann was there, too, and Shelly. And in various conversations, the two of them continued to be my voice when the many words I was attempting became too much.

I encountered many people throughout the week who are trying to be a voice for those who have none. Not just speaking for a feverish friend with laryngitis, but speaking for the beleaguered and weary, the disenfranchised who cannot speak for themselves or who speak and are never heard. I met people who speak out for orphans; I talked with two women about their vision for connecting people who have been hurt by the church; and I sat across from a new friend who has a heart for families struggling through infertility and the church struggling toward diversity and reconciliation. And there were so many others.

By the time I got home, my voice was nearly back to normal, though even now, a week and a half later, I find the raspiness returning in the mornings and evenings. I gulp down cough syrup to prevent the hacking, and I swallow pills to abate the pain.

But receiving my voice back has become less a medical issue and more a heart issue. Quieting the vocal chords requires quieting my spirit, and listening better is a habit I need to grow into.

FarawayNearby
December 9

began my day in the dark, and in the dark I will enter
the death of sleep once more. Each day is a journey from
dark to dark. But in the middle, the light.

It's the light that shines from one direction or the other
and reveals to us where we are, where we will be. The
shadows of light indicate whether we are coming or going.
The brightness of the light tells how long until we get there.
The proximity of light tells us whether we are faraway or
nearby. From dawn to midday to dusk. We are here. We are
there. We are here again.

Recently, when I should have been here, I've been there.
When I should have been there, I've been here. I have
confused the faraway and the nearby. Partly because there
is so little light. Mostly because I have covered the light and
let so little of it shine. In the nearby, it's hard to see the
faraway. In the faraway, the nearby is unrecognizable.

Only the light sees them both. The Light is the
Faraway-Nearby.

In Georgia O'Keeffe's painting *From the Faraway,
Nearby*, she plays with the light and its perspective; she
removes size and scale as relative; she focuses the Faraway
and Nearby in equal proportions. The enormous animal
skull and the rolling foothills share space as if the viewer is

both here and there at the same time. The artist depicted both objects with such detailed realism I trust the painting more than my eyes. Something seems wrong. It must be me.

But even the skull possesses too many antlers to be real. The bifurcation of the sky, too distinct. The mountains, too smooth. This wasn't just about the antlers or the mountains. This was about the faraway, "a beautiful, untouched lonely-feeling place," O'Keeffe wrote[1], and about the nearby, and not about the middle place where too often we get lost, even in the light.

"To love someone is to put yourself in their place, we say, which is to put yourself in their story," writes Rebecca Solnit, in her book *The Faraway Nearby*, named after O'Keeffe's painting. "Which means that a place is a story, and stories are geography, and empathy is first of all an act of imagination, a storyteller's art, and then a way of traveling from here to there."[2]

And that's what I've been missing as I muddle through the dim light of the middle place. Without empathy I am neither faraway – in your story – or nearby – in my story. I am stuck, and the light makes things seem so real, but they aren't.

That's why the Faraway-Nearby, the true Light, had to come close, to incarnate, to empathize, because otherwise, we would never find our place in His story, and the traveling from here to there would be very far indeed.

It's as Joseph Brodsky writes in his "Star of the Nativity." The star is "from far away – from the depth of the universe," but also "from its opposite end.[3]"

The Faraway-Nearby came near then far. We are here. We are there.

God with us.

Away
December 16

For someone who works at home, I've spent a lot of time away from the nest over the past few weeks. A 10-day trip to Texas kicked off a busy season of workshops and book signings, of family obligations and medical appointments, of cooking and shopping and celebrating.

From last Thursday evening until just last night, my brief times at home were spent sleeping and preparing to leave again. And in that short stint, land was auctioned, and a loved one laid to rest. Relationships were restored, and old friends reacquainted. Books were sold, and Christmas gifts purchased. I celebrated the season with friends and dreaded the results of medical tests. I cooked and ate and loved and worked.

And drove. Lots and lots of driving.

I don't like being away much. I also don't much like being away. Being away a lot leaves me tired, disconnected, languishing.

During Advent, I've thought a lot about away-ness, how during this middle time of waiting for Jesus to come again that he's the one who's away.

But in truth, it's not Jesus who's away. It's me. The wistfulness of the holiday season, the dashed expectations, the longing for more even in the excess: these are the symptoms of homesickness. And I am the one who's far from home. Advent longing stirs deeper than just a return visit with Jesus. I long for him to come back and take me with him. To take us all home where we belong.

Maybe that's the real beauty of the holiday season. That's the reason things never quite go the way we want or plan. Because no matter where we spend Christmas, we are away from the home we were made for.

I have a few more rides in the car, a few more trips away from home before the New Year is born. And the time away will get harder, not easier.

But the comforts of home keep me going and coming, and the Promise of Home keeps me hoping and believing.

And those medical tests I was dreading? They all came out just fine. Again. And I am thankful.

Users Guide

How can just one word make a difference? By choosing a word each week, you take time to reflect, imagine, pray, anticipate. When you choose just one word, you narrow down, synthesize, encapsulate, prioritize. Over time, the words help you see what's been going on in your life, where God has been at work, what your fears and dreams led you to do. Here are a few tips for starting your own word of the week project:

How to pick your word
- Think about your week.
- Consider what's behind, what's ahead, what you dread, and what you anticipate.
- Consider what words might describe your activities and your feelings.
- If you have many things going on, create a venn diagram and see where they overlap.
- Choose a word that will help you focus and engage with what's really going on.

How to use your word
- Journal about it.
- Pray over it.
- Share it in a group.
- Write it out on a sticky note in your car.
- Share it on Charity's weekly Facebook thread.
- Research your word or pick a synonym, then write a blog post about it each week.

Interact with others
- Ask your kids for their word at dinner.
- Talk about your word with your spouse or friends.
- Use #wordoftheweek as an icebreaker in a meeting.
- Each week ask one member of your team to share their word.
- Ask others to pick a word for you based on what they know about your life.

Keep track of your words
- Write down your word of the week for a whole year (consider using the following pages).
- Notice duplicates.
- Observe themes.
- Type your words in a single document and create a Wordle.
- Journal about the year-long experience of choosing a word every week.

Week 1

Word:_____

Notes: _____

_____

Week 2

Word:_____

Notes: _____

_____

Week 3

Word:_____

Notes: _____

_____

Week 4

Word:_____

Notes: _____

_____

Week 5

Word:_____

Notes: _____

_____

Week 6

Word:_____

Notes: _____

_____

Week 7

Word: _____

Notes: _____

_____

Week 8

Word: _____

Notes: _____

_____

Week 9

Word: _____

Notes: _____

_____

Week 10

Word: _____

Notes: _____

_____

Week 11

Word: _____

Notes: _____

_____

Week 12

Word: _____

Notes: _____

_____

Week 13

Word:_____

Notes: _____

_____

Week 14

Word:_____

Notes: _____

_____

Week 15

Word:_____

Notes: _____

_____

Week 16

Word:_____

Notes: _____

_____

Week 17

Word:_____

Notes: _____

_____

Week 18

Word:_____

Notes: _____

_____

Week 19

Word: _____

Notes: _____

_____

Week 20

Word: _____

Notes: _____

_____

Week 21

Word: _____

Notes: _____

_____

Week 22

Word: _____

Notes: _____

_____

Week 23

Word: _____

Notes: _____

_____

Week 24

Word: _____

Notes: _____

_____

Week 25

Word:_____

Notes: _____

_____

Week 26

Word:_____

Notes: _____

_____

Week 27

Word:_____

Notes: _____

_____

Week 28

Word:_____

Notes: _____

_____

Week 29

Word:_____

Notes: _____

_____

Week 30

Word:_____

Notes: _____

_____

Week 31

Word: _____

Notes:_____

_____

Week 32

Word: _____

Notes:_____

_____

Week 33

Word: _____

Notes:_____

_____

Week 34

Word: _____

Notes:_____

_____

Week 35

Word: _____

Notes:_____

_____

Week 36

Word: _____

Notes:_____

_____

Week 37

Word:_____

Notes: _____

Week 38

Word:_____

Notes: _____

Week 39

Word:_____

Notes: _____

Week 40

Word:_____

Notes: _____

Week 41

Word:_____

Notes: _____

Week 42

Word:_____

Notes: _____

Week 43

Word:_____

Notes:_____

_____

Week 44

Word:_____

Notes:_____

_____

Week 45

Word:_____

Notes:_____

_____

Week 46

Word:_____

Notes:_____

_____

Week 47

Word:_____

Notes:_____

_____

Week 48

Word:_____

Notes:_____

_____

Week 49

Word:_____

Notes: _____

_____

Week 50

Word:_____

Notes: _____

_____

Week 51

Word:_____

Notes: _____

_____

Week 52

Word:_____

Notes: _____

_____

Acknowledgements

No book is possible without a team of people supporting the author.

Thank you to my readers who have commented and joined in on my word of the week project for several years now. Your encouragement bolsters me.

Thank you to the many writers who have joined me by writing an "In Your Own Words" post on my blog. Your words inspire me.

Thank you to Ann Kroeker for being my coauthor, collaborator, colleague, and friend. My writing life is so much richer with you in it.

Thank you to Laura Barkat, LW Lindquist, Glynn Young, Richard Maxson, Heather Eure, Ann Kroeker (again!), and the whole Tweetspeak Poetry family for creating, sustaining, and inviting us all into such a nurturing and motivating writing community. I write better because of you.

Thank you to the many friends and family who share their lives (and therefore their stories) with me.

Thank you to Nicholas, Caleb, and Jacob who make my life more fun and funnier. I love you all.

And lastly, thank you to Steven who always makes room in our lives for my words. Love you always.

End Notes

Human
[1] Weintraub, Karen. "Researchers turn adult cells back into stem cells." *USA Today.* 29 January 2014. Web. 21 July 2016.
[2] ibid.

Simple
[1] Microsoft Excel is a registered trademark of the Microsoft group.
[2] The workshop is long since passed, but you can check out other workshops at TweetspeakPoetry.com/category/workshops/.

Presbyopia
[1]"Diseases and Conditions: Presbyopia." Mayo Clinic. Mayo Foundation for Medical Education and Research. 17 October 2014. Web. 21 July 2016.
[2]"Frequently asked questions." Casey Eye Institute. Oregon Health & Science University. Web. 21 July 2016.
[3] Scripture quotations taken from the New American Standard Bible® (NASB), Copyright © 1960, 1962, 1963, 1968, 1971, 1972, 1973,1975, 1977, 1995 by The Lockman Foundation. Used by permission. www.Lockman.org.

Connected

[1] DeRusha, Michelle. *Spiritual Misfit: A Memoir of Uneasy Faith*. New York: Convergent Books, 2014. Print.
[2] DeRusha, 134.
[3] Ibid.
[4] DeRusha, 137.

Preapproved

[1] Lee, Jennifer Dukes. *Love Idol: Letting Go of Your Need for Approval – and Seeing Yourself through God's Eyes*. Carol Stream, Ill.: Tyndale Momentum, 2014. Print.
[2] Lee, xvii-xviii.

Mastery

[1] Clear, James. "How the 'Seinfeld Strategy' Can Help You Stop Procrastinating." *Entrepreneur*. 27 January 2014. Web. 29 July 2016.
[2] Ramsey, Russ. "A World Short on Masters." *The Rabbit Room*. May 2011. Web. 29 July 2016.
[3] Rupert, David. "Moving Beyond Mediocrity: Playing It Safe Will Never Change the World." *The High Calling*. 31 March 2014. Web. 29 July 2016.
[4] Khang, Kathy. "Moving Beyond Mediocrity: You Are Worth It." *The High Calling*. 2 April 2014. Web. 29 July 2016.
[5] Cyzewski, Ed. "Moving Beyond Mediocrity: Asking Yourself the Tough Questions." 1 April 2014. Web. 29 July 2016.
[6] Day, Charles. "The Four Weapons of Exceptional Creative Leaders." *Fast Company*. 18 June 2013. Web. 29 July 2016.
[7] Ibid.

Preapproved
[1] DeRusha, Michelle. *Spiritual Misfit: A Memoir of Uneasy Faith.* New York: Convergent Books, 2014. 127. Print.
[2] DeRusha, 99.

Wind
[1] Scripture quotations taken from the New American Standard Bible® (NASB), Copyright © 1960, 1962, 1963, 1968, 1971, 1972, 1973, 1975, 1977, 1995 by The Lockman Foundation. Used by permission. www.Lockman.org.

Growth
[1] The Square Foot Gardening method was invented by Mel Bartholomew in 1981. See http://www.squarefootgardening.com/.

Scarcity
[1] Bessey, Sarah. "Rethinking Scarcity: The Legacy of Abundance." The High Calling. 22 June 2014. Web. 2 August 2016.
[2] Ibid.
[3] Ibid.

Friendship
[1] Andrews, Amy, and Jessica Mesman Griffith. *Love & Salt: A Spiritual Friendship Shared in Letters.* Chicago: Loyala Press, 2013. 236. Print.
[2] Ibid.
[3] Andrews, 238.

Revelation
[1] Keller, Tim. *Counterfeit Gods: The Empty Promises of Money, Sex, and Power, and the Only Hope that Matters.* New York, Dutton: 2009. eBook.

Deadline
[1] That book eventually became *On Being a Writer: 12 Simple Habits for a Writing Life that Lasts* by Ann Kroeker and Charity Singleton Craig (October 2014, TS Poetry Press).

Capacity
[1] Kroeker, Ann. *Not So Fast: Slow-down Solutions for Frenzied Families*. Colorado Springs: David C. Cook, 2009. 126. Print.
[2] Kroeker, 130.

Improvise
[1] Pershey, Katherine Willis. "Yes, And ..." *Katherine Willis Pershey: Writer, Pastor, Raconteuse*. 12 July 2014. Web. 3 August 2016.
[2] Fey, Tina. *Bossypants*. New York: Little Brown and Company, 2011. ebook.

Dust
[1] Scripture quotations taken from the New American Standard Bible® (NASB), Copyright © 1960, 1962, 1963, 1968, 1971, 1972, 1973, 1975, 1977, 1995 by The Lockman Foundation. Used by permission. www.Lockman.org.

Juggle
[1] Weinschenk, Susan, Ph.D. "The True Cost Of Multi-Tasking." *Psychology Today*. 18 September 2012. Web. 3 August 1, 2016.

Settled
[1] Scripture quotations taken from the New American Standard Bible® (NASB), Copyright © 1960, 1962, 1963, 1968, 1971, 1972, 1973, 1975, 1977, 1995 by The Lockman Foundation. Used by permission. www.Lockman.org.

Play

[1] *The Voice* is owned by NBC Universal.

Happy

[1] Apparently, there has been much discussion and debate about the true authorship of the Serenity Prayer. *The Yale Alumni* magazine has a full article about the origin and attributes the article to Reinhold Niebuhr. Read more at "Who Wrote the Serenity Prayer?" at the http://archives.yalealumnimagazine.com/issues/2008_07/ser enity.html.

[2] Scripture quotations taken from the New American Standard Bible® (NASB), Copyright © 1960, 1962, 1963, 1968, 1971, 1972, 1973, 1975, 1977, 1995 by The Lockman Foundation. Used by permission. www.Lockman.org.

FarawayNearby

[1] Scanlan, Laura Wolff. "Ghost Ranch and the Faraway Nearby." *Humanities*. July/August 2009. Web. 3 August 2016.

[2] Solnit, Rebecca. *The Faraway Nearby*. New York: Penguin, 2013. eBook.

[3] Brodsky, Joseph "Star of the Nativity." *Collected Poems in English, 1972-1999*. New York: Farrar Straus and Giroux, 2000.